NORTH
STAR
WAY

MORE ADVANCE PRAISE FOR
50 WAYS TO YAY!

"Alexi is the next generation of thought leader, paving a path with her incredibly unique and down-to-earth approach. Alexi's insights and tools to uncovering personal happiness and freedom will leave you inspired and empowered to take action in all areas of your life!"

—Jack Canfield, author of the #1 *New York Times* bestselling Chicken Soup for the Soul® series and *The Success Principles*™

"If you want to go from 'blah' to 'YAY!' this book is your guide. An uplifting read with stories to inspire confidence and action steps to take to actually change. Alexi is the perfect mix of the encouraging best friend you can't live without and the cool teacher you always wanted. She offers you simple yet powerful ways to stop making excuses and start creating your own happiness."

—Christine Hassler, author of *Expectation Hangover*

"Alexi Panos is a force of positivity in a world that so desperately needs a nudge. Inspiring and motivating, this book offers practical reflections and exercises so you can treat every day with the intention and purpose it deserves."

—Adam Smiley Poswolsky,
author of *The Quarter-Life Breakthrough*

"Alexi Panos is to this generation what Debbie Ford and Marianne Williamson are to past generations."

—Jake Ducey, author of *The Purpose Principles*

"I am extremely excited for the world to experience her magic in this book. What she's done here is create a resource that will allow you to finish and implement easily to create an experience that can and will change your life. Brava, Alexi!"

—Elizabeth DiAlto, author of *Untame Yourself: Reconnect to the Lost Art, Power, and Freedom of Being a Woman*

"I loved the no-nonsense, workbook-style approach in *50 Ways to Yay*. It's truly life-altering!

-Light Watkins, author of *The Inner Gym*

"An A+ read! If you follow this book the way Alexi has laid it out for you, you will see your life explode with happiness and peace of mind."

—Ben Altman, editor of *Charisma on Command*

50 WAYS TO YAY!

Transformative Tools for
a Whole Lot of Happy

ALEXI PANOS

NORTH STAR WAY

New York   London   Toronto   Sydney   New Delhi

NORTH
STAR
WAY

North Star Way
An Imprint of Simon & Schuster, Inc.
1230 Avenue of the Americas
New York, NY 10020

First North Star Way paperback edition June 2016

NORTH STAR WAY and colophon are registered trademarks of Simon & Schuster, Inc.

For information about special discounts for bulk purchases, please contact Simon & Schuster Special Sales at 1-866-506-1949 or business@simonandschuster.com.

The North Star Way Speakers Bureau can bring authors to your live event. For more information or to book an event, contact the North Star Way Speakers Bureau at 1-212-698-8888 or visit our website at www.thenorthstarway.com.

Interior design by Jaime Putorti

Manufactured in the United States of America

10 9 8 7 6 5 4 3 2 1

ISBN 978-1-5011-3178-3
ISBN 978-1-5011-3179-0 (ebook)

This book is dedicated to YOU. You are one of the special ones. You want something more out of life; you want to squeeze all of the juice from it, and THAT gets me excited. I get to live my passion because YOU are passionate about living. I can't thank you enough for your dedication to being awesome and ultimately making our world a better place by sharing all that goodness in you.

You seriously rock.

xo
Alexi

CONTENTS

READ THIS FIRST!

Throughout my twenties, I was living what most would call a successful life: I was easily earning a healthy six-figure income as a model and television host, creating my own schedule, traveling the world, and having the ability to pour my free time and money into my own nonprofit work in Africa. But something was still missing. While I seemingly had it all, I felt out of alignment with who I truly was on the inside.

So I began studying the great masters in psychology, philosophy, personal development, and neuroscience; taking countless workshops and classes; and digesting as many books as I could get my hands on. I made sure to keep an open mind with every lesson I learned; I applied each to my own life first, and then decided whether it felt right for me to incorporate into my beliefs. Through years of experimenting with different thought traditions and mental technologies, I have created my own version of the "best of the best" within this book, which is fifty of the personal exercises that I use on a daily basis to check in with myself, hold myself accountable, and ultimately uncover happiness in this beautiful life that we get to live.

I made this book as fun and easy to digest as I could, so that you can actually TAKE ACTION and experience the results that you're truly after. You can choose to go chronologically through the book, starting at Lesson 1 and ending at Lesson 50, or you can flip through and randomly select a lesson each day. Whichever way you choose, I highly recommend doing fifty consistent days of exercises in order to create a new pattern within your brain to see the world differently. It's been proven, time and time again, that if you want to incorporate new, powerful habits, you must consistently stick with the practice. And remember, we get out of life what we put INTO it, so doing the work is critical if you want results.

Finishing a book cover to cover is an amazing accomplishment, but putting the theory into action is where your life actually transforms. The beauty of self-discovery is that it is a never-ending process. Each of us is a new person every day, so the same lesson can offer new insights again and again. Life will continue to barrage us with new circumstances, and with these tools in your arsenal you'll be ready to meet them head-on. We could read a book about tennis all day, but until we get on the court and actually practice serving the ball, it's all theory. The same goes for human development. We are SO very complex, and there is SO much to learn about mastering our personal potential; but until we put it into action, it's all just a bunch of ideas floating around in our heads. Keep coming back to it and make it a daily practice until it becomes second nature to you.

It's my heartfelt passion to inspire others to step fully into their greatness, to live lives so abundantly beautiful and filled with love that their hearts overflow with joy into the lives of others. I'm committed to that, and I want to sincerely thank you for your commitment to yourself—it's the first step to truly changing the planet.

50
WAYS
TO
YAY!

In order to SEE the change, we must BE the change.

#50WaysToYay

1. LET'S CHANGE THE WORLD, SHALL WE?

The great poet Rumi has given us these wise words: "Yesterday I was clever, so I wanted to change the world. Today I am wise, so I am changing myself." When we change, the world around us changes. When we work on being the most amazing version of ourselves, on transforming our hearts and our minds, we can let that goodness ripple out and affect the world. We all have the power to change and transform ourselves, and when we realize this truth, we can bring forth that power into every circumstance we encounter.

Many of us are anxious to improve our circumstances, but we're reluctant to improve ourselves; we want the incredible life, but we don't want to do the work. We can't change the world until we're willing to change ourselves, because ultimately our view of the world is a direct reflection of how we're personally showing up in it. In any situation where we feel something is lacking, it's usually something within ourselves that is missing from the equation. Sure, it's easy to look at the world around us and blame it for all of our misfortunes, but placing the blame outside ourselves doesn't bring us any closer to actually solving the problem.

Whether we're feeling a lack of love, of financial security, of intimacy, or of peace in our lives, the solution can usually be found within ourselves. If we dig deep enough, get brutally honest, and take responsibility for how WE'RE showing up under those circumstances, we can see that external things are not to blame; instead, it is what we're not willing to GIVE to the situation.

I used to feel a lack of intimacy in my relationships. I felt as though my partner and friends weren't opening up fully or sharing their true feelings. It wasn't until I realized that I wasn't showing up fully open, vulnerable, and willing to share that I could understand that I was the missing ingredient. When I began to shift, my reality shifted with me. I dropped my walls and began to show up as ALL of me, and people who weren't meant for my life gradually fell out of it, while I formed deeper relationships with those who stayed. My relationships expanded exponentially the more I revealed who I truly was, and suddenly that lack of intimacy I had once felt became a distant memory.

If we want to experience more love, we have to choose to be love. If we want to experience more abundance, we have to be the embodiment of that abundance. If we want to experience peace, we have to practice it first. We don't get what we want, we get what we ARE. So whatever it is that you feel you're lacking in life, get brutally honest with yourself and ask how you are showing up to it. We will receive and attract into our lives only what we are willing to BE, and what we feel we're missing is a direct indicator of where we're not giving enough of ourselves.

YOUR MISSION: In what area of your life do you most dislike the results you're getting? (Relationships, career/purpose, money, health, spirituality, lifestyle, etc.)

_____

_____

Who or what do you need to become in order to get the results you desire in this area?

_____

_____

_____

_____

REFLECTION: How does it feel knowing that you are 100 percent responsible for your experience of life? Do you feel more empowered and confident in the face of the inevitable adversity that will show up?

_____

_____

_____

_____

_____

_____

_____

_____

2. NOTHING REQUIRED

Those who are happy with nothing are happy with everything. If we allow the external world to be the source of our happiness, we'll never feel truly fulfilled. At best, the novelty of what is "new" will eventually wear off, and we'll inevitably be searching for the next best thing to make us feel better. At worst, we lose the object or person we attached our happiness to, and we feel like we lost a part of our identity in the process.

Defining our worth by our titles, possessions, situations, relationships, and accomplishments is a surefire path toward powerlessness, because external objects are always subject to change. We may lose our job, our relationship may suddenly change direction, we may never get that title we were hoping for, or we could physically damage or lose items we possess. As long as our sense of self-worth is tied to something outside of ourselves, our life will feel unstable and full of uncertainty.

So how can we create a sense of control in an unstable world? Instead of identifying with the changing nature of objects or events, we must identify with our true nature—our core essence. Core essence? What the heck does that mean? I like to think of our core essence like the Universe—it's the limitless, infinite, and incredibly powerful container for everything. There is all the stuff that's in the Universe: dark matter, galaxies, planets, and everything on each of those planets. That stuff, while a critical part of the Universe, is simply just a *part* of it, and it's always in flux. Our titles, our accomplishments, our cars, our relationships, and our things are like the ever-changing objects within the Universe. The problem is, most of us are identifying ourselves by the stuff that's passing through our experience rather than identifying with our true, unchanging core essence; therefore, we feel restless, anxious, and worried about what's next.

No matter what craziness may be happening in our external world, we can rely on the deep, unchanging core of who we are that always feels capable, joyful, and worthy; the self that was enough when we were born into this world with nothing, and will continue to be enough when we leave this world with nothing.

When we trust the eternal "enoughness" of our core essence, we are released from the need for approval from others, and ultimately our desire for and attachment to stuff fades away. We then begin to realize that happiness and security are an inside job, and we can choose to feel these emotions at any given time. That's when a deep sense of inner peace shows up because we can move through the world without feeling compelled to try to control it. So bask in the richness and completeness of the real, core YOU—and you will find happiness was always just a choice away.

YOUR MISSION: What was one thing you were excited about when you first obtained it: a new purse, a fancy job title, your home, your car, a new electronic device or appliance?

_____

_____

_____

Think about how the novelty wore off and how you've moved on to procuring other things. Just become aware of how quickly your initial excitement faded.

REFLECTION: If you lost all of your possessions, what would you be left with that would mean the world to you? What would you be grateful for?

_____

_____

_____

_____

_____

_____

_____

_____

If you have listed people who are dear to you above, call them right now and tell them how much they mean to you.

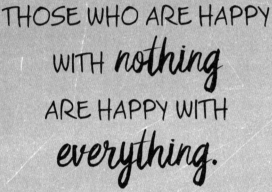

THOSE WHO ARE HAPPY
WITH *nothing*
ARE HAPPY WITH
everything.

#50WaysToYay

3. YOU ARE A MASTER

We are all masters of manifesting. We are in fact manifesting everything in our lives at every given moment. Wherever we are right now, whatever our lives look like, WE have actually brought it all into our experience. Every thought we have, every desire that lives deep inside of us, every fear and insecurity that sleeps just below the surface radiates a frequency that attracts a matching frequency back, eventually becoming the experiences of our lives. And yes, this means both the good AND the bad (yikes!).

Our subconscious mind is essentially the director of the film that our conscious mind views as our day-to-day experiences; the problem is, we're also the scriptwriter. Unfortunately, our scriptwriter is our inner eight-year-old who is lacing each and every script passed through our conscious mind with beliefs that we adopted from our early childhood. These beliefs were established after we identified or associated with both negative experiences (in order to keep us "safe" from ever experiencing them again) and positive ones (in order to know what we can trust). We write this script from our innermost dialogue of these subconscious beliefs, and the director (our subconscious mind) takes the material as is and brings it to our reality. The script plays itself out and ultimately attracts and manifests more of the same back into the next version of our script, strengthening and reaffirming these beliefs.

Sometimes those actions and dialogues are positive, joyful, and loving, so we get exponentially more of that in our lives. Sometimes our scripts are filled with fear, scarcity, and distrust, which attracts more and more of what we say we don't want.

So how do we override this cycle? The key is AWARE-NESS. Once we become aware that at every given moment we are creating our reality, we can then pay attention to our innermost thoughts and feelings, and begin to get intentional with our thoughts and actions and focus them on what we want.

Esther and Jerry Hicks spoke a bit about this in *Ask and It Is Given*, their classic book on the law of attraction: "You can literally script any life that you desire, and the Universe will deliver to you the people, the places, and events just as you decide them to be. For you are a creator of your own experience—you have only to decide it and allow it to be." As our thoughts and actions shift, we shift what information the scriptwriter uses, therefore shifting the type of film we watch play out as our reality. So if you find yourself complaining about what's not working, be prepared to get more of what's not working. If you find yourself being grateful for what is working, get ready to embrace all of the abundance of good coming your way. The hard truth is, if we want to experience a different reality than the one we're in now, we need to start paying attention to our thoughts, feelings, ways of being, and, most important, our actions. It ALL matters, and you're the one calling the shots.

YOUR MISSION: What in your life is not working right now?

_____

_____

What subconscious beliefs may have been responsible for attracting this into your life?

_____

_____

_____

_____

What in your life IS working right now?

_____

_____

What subconscious beliefs may have been responsible for attracting this into your life?

_____

_____

REFLECTION: Now that you're aware of the power of your subconscious belief systems, what actions will you take to begin to override the negative cycle?

_____

_____

_____

_____

_____

EVERYTHING IN YOUR LIFE,
good and bad,
WAS MANIFESTED
by YOU.

#50WaysToYay

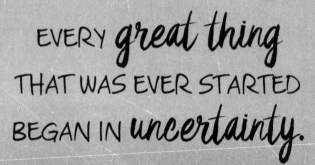

EVERY *great thing* THAT WAS EVER STARTED BEGAN IN *uncertainty.*

#50WaysToYay

4. EVERYTHING STARTS WITH UNCERTAINTY

Every great thing that was ever started began in uncertainty. Thomas Alva Edison asked, "Will this work?" and now we experience the gift of the lightbulb. Steve Jobs pondered, "Is there a need for this?" and now we have minicomputers that fit in our pockets. In order to bring our ideas or dreams to life, we have to expect fear and uncertainty, welcome it in, and know that once we face it, it no longer has a hold on us. We must remind ourselves that there are two possible ends to every uncertain journey we embark upon: either we learn a lesson that brings us one step closer to our true desires or we reach the point we set out for. I don't know about you, but those odds sound pretty darn good.

Unfortunately, most of us avoid our fears by staying in our comfort zones and refusing to stretch ourselves. We avoid our fears, and in turn, our fears grow bigger and bigger every time we let fear win. A great example of this from my own life is public speaking. I used to have what I would call a pretty normal fear of speaking to crowds; I stayed away from public speaking for years and years because of it. I would get asked to speak about my nonprofit work or to share my personal story and I would say no to about 65 percent of the opportunities that came my way. Every time I said no, I let fear win. That fear eventually became so overwhelming that I began getting physical reactions at the mere mention of speaking to an audience: my palms would sweat, my heart rate would quicken, and my entire body would go on high alert.

The more I grew my business, the more I knew that speaking would be an integral part of it. I knew that, despite the loud voice of my inner fear, I had to face it, welcome it in with a smile, and work with it if I wanted to continue to make a big impact. Now I continually acknowledge the fear (hello there, old friend!), and do what I'm afraid of doing anyway. I recognize my fear when it decides to show up, wave at it, breathe deeply through it, and say, "Let's do this!" I put myself in the speaking arena constantly, and practice getting out of my head (where my fear lives) and getting into my body by being present with my breath. With every opportunity I have to talk before an audience, my fear gets smaller and smaller, and that comes with the practice of pushing past it.

In order to fly, we must be willing to give up the ground we're used to standing on. In order to catch the view from the top, we must be willing to let go and soar. We can't expect to get from Point A (where our lives are now) to Point B (where we want them to be) if we're not willing to give up Point A. Yes, we will absolutely have setbacks along the way, but if we never take that leap, we'll never know what it feels like to truly fly in life. If we're too committed to our comfort, we'll never feel the power of fully letting go and spreading our wings.

If we want progress in any area of our lives, we must anticipate a certain amount of risk, which will inevitably bring some fear into play. If you're not experiencing *any* fear, then you're probably not stretching yourself enough. Often our greatness lies just on the other side of our fear, uncertainty, and comfort zone, so we can use fear as an indicator that points us to areas that could potentially accelerate our greatness. By consistently choosing to act despite the fear, we give ourselves the opportunity to create true greatness in our lives.

So it's time to risk your comfort for true happiness. It's time to take that leap that you KNOW will set your heart on fire. Don't miss all the good stuff because you are unwilling to let go out of fear. Don't let the fear that you're holding on to hold you back from the life of your dreams. Remember, we'll never know what we're truly capable of if we never give it a shot.

YOUR MISSION: What is one idea, project, or desired outcome that you've been putting off?

_____

_____

What result or outcome are you most afraid of?

_____

_____

What is ONE SMALL STEP you can take RIGHT NOW that would bring you closer to your vision and force you to move through the fear?

_____

_____

DO IT. Right now! No, seriously. Stop this and DO IT.

REFLECTION: How does it feel to honestly look at WHY you've been putting this off? How does it feel to know you're one step closer?

_____

_____

_____

_____

_____

_____

_____

_____

_____

_____

_____

5. HOW DO YOU DEFINE SUCCESS?

Defining success on our own terms may be one of the most important things we can do in life. So many of us have been programmed by well-meaning adults and society to believe that success involves a particular kind of career, romantic partner, belief system, and lifestyle. Most of us have been in the habit of doing things to make others happy for so long that we've become completely numb to our own desires. When we're not clear on how *we* define success, how can we ever expect to feel successful? Well, it's time to take back our lives and honor what truly matters to us.

Your job today is to simply define what success looks like to you. Once you have a clear idea of how you define success, you can begin taking actions toward that vision, and the HOW will start to unfold.

YOUR MISSION: Get clear on what the term "success" means to you in each area below. What does it ideally look like for you; what words would describe it?

Relationships: _____
_____

Career: _____
_____

Health/Body: _____

_____

Lifestyle: _____

_____

Finances: _____

_____

Possessions: _____

_____

Personal Growth/Spirituality: _____

_____

REFLECTION: How does it feel to clearly define success on YOUR terms?

_____

_____

_____

_____

What actions are you inspired to take to move you closer to a life of your choosing?

_____

_____

_____

_____

CREATE
YOUR OWN
definition
of
success.

#50WaysToYay

SHOW UP AS
LOVE
IN THE ABSENCE OF IT.

#50WaysToYay

6. THE TWO EMOTIONS

Countless spiritual texts touch on the principle that there are only two core emotions, love and fear, and that all other emotions are simply variants on these two. Fear shows up as anxiety, shame, anger, sadness, depression, the need to control, jealousy, inadequacy, loneliness, hurt, and guilt. Love shows up as acceptance, forgiveness, happiness, trust, compassion, appreciation, care, truthfulness, satisfaction, and joy. If there are only these two core emotions, then fear is simply the absence of love. So if we're experiencing an emotional state related to fear and want out of it, all we need to do is bring in an emotional state related to love in order to override it.

TURN ON THE LIGHT

I like to think of the emotions of love as light and those of fear as darkness. The only way to get rid of darkness is by bringing in the light. Often, when we're faced with these dark emotions, our ego tries to combat them with more darkness, but that doesn't work. We can't meet anger with anger, hate with hate, or even jealousy with frustration and expect to get a positive result. When we meet darkness with darkness, we're just making an already dark room even blacker.

The ONLY way to rid our emotional rooms of the darkness that's in them is to bring in the LIGHT with love, compassion, empathy, joy, affection, courage, humility, appreciation, peace, support, and gratitude. This is such a simple concept, but one that takes courage and humility to put into practice. I'm constantly challenging myself to show up as light in the face of darkness, no matter how much my ego tries to resist it, because it really does work.

Before I learned about this lesson, I would engage in disagreements with loved ones in a very stubborn way: "I'm right [pride and defensiveness] and I will do whatever it takes to prove it to you [anger, fear of being wrong or judged, and frustration]." As you can imagine, this approach didn't get me very far; in fact, I destroyed a lot of relationships using it. Now, when I'm able to catch myself falling into old patterns, I bring awareness to the situation and realize that the only way to come to a place of peace and unity (light) is to BE the light. Instead of pride and defensiveness, I show up with understanding. In place of anger, frustration, and fear, I invite in love, peace, and compassion. Inevitably, the moment I turn on my light, I am able to dispel some of that unwanted darkness; and the brighter my light shines, the quicker that darkness fades away.

We must be brave enough to show up as LOVE in the face of hurt, as COURAGE in the face of fear, and as COMPASSION in the face of hate. With the power of our awareness, we humans have this crazy ability to be able to rise above the darkness in life by simply CHOOSING to do so. It's not easy—in fact, it goes against everything we've been programmed to do since childhood—but love is always just a choice away. We all have the light within us, a little bulb just waiting to be switched on, but it takes a conscious choice to flip the switch and shine when we're faced with some of life's darkest moments.

Start today by asking yourself: Do I choose to turn on my light? If not, what am I afraid of seeing in myself or in others? Who am I not willing to be? What is that costing me? If you're already rocking your light, ask yourself: How can I brighten it? How can I share my shine with more people?

Life is short; flip that light switch and SHINE ON.

YOUR MISSION: Get honest. Are you a person who spends most of your time in the light (empowering, uplifting, and loving emotions and conversations) or in the dark (negative, disempowering, and fearful emotions and conversations)?

_____

_____

Are you a dimmer or a brightener for others in your life?

_____

_____

Today, commit to shining your light, especially when it's uncomfortable. Notice when a situation comes up and you feel yourself wanting to react with darkness (fear, frustration, impatience, anger, jealousy, etc.); ask how you can shine your light, your LOVE, on that situation. What emotion of love could you bring forth that would dispel the darkness that you're feeling?

REFLECTION: What did this exercise open up for you? How did consciously turning on your inner light in the face of challenges change the experience of your day?

_____

_____

_____

_____

_____

_____

_____

_____

7. IT'S ALL FOR YOU

It didn't happen TO you, it happened FOR you. Every single step on your journey was ESSENTIAL in evolving you into the person you are today. Your spirit called in these experiences so that you could learn, grow, and expand into the highest version of yourself. Who you are today is a direct reflection of every single good, bad, ugly, and amazing thing that has ever happened to you; and who you will be five years from now will require you to persevere through all that you are currently up against.

Yes, sometimes we're not dealt the best hand with which to play the game of life. But these cards are the only ones we've got. So what are we going to do about it? Are we going to give up, fold, and complain about the cards we were dealt? Or are we going to make magic with the hand we've been given? Our level of happiness has little to do with the hand itself and everything to do with how we choose to play it. It's not about our lack of resources; it's about how resourceful we are. It's not about our circumstances—it's about whom we show up as in the face of them. Complaining about the hand we've been dealt is a painful path that leads nowhere fast and produces zero results along the way.

We must powerfully forgive and leave behind our past, because when we bring our past with us into the current moment, we will never be fully present to what's happening NOW. It's like spending an evening with friends obsessing about something that you said at the beginning of the night, thus missing all the juicy stuff that happens along the way. If we want to create a brand-new painting of our lives, we should probably start with a brand-spanking-new canvas. We COULD always paint over the old one, but the colors will never be as bright as they could be.

So whatever you experienced that brought you here, forgive it and know that it didn't happen TO you; rather, it happened FOR your highest good. Release your past and be grateful for all of the people and experiences that have contributed to your evolution as a human being. Realize that whatever is present right now is perfect for the continued unfolding of your life.

RADICAL RESPONSIBILITY

If we want to actualize our potential, create lasting happiness, and become the most energized, abundant, joyful, and present human beings we can be, we must learn to be radically responsible. We are the sole authors of our lives; therefore, we must take 100 percent ownership for what's working AND what's not working with our health, finances, career, relationships, lifestyle, feelings, results or lack thereof. ALL OF IT IS UP TO US.

If your life isn't working, it's not your life, it's YOU. If you're feeling overwhelmed, stressed-out, broke, lonely, stalled-out, and you are not living up to your potential, the only person responsible for this is YOU. Either we CAUSE something or we ALLOW it. We are the problem, but we are also the solution. While this lesson is a hard truth to hear, it is a necessary one.

All events are neutral; it's how we respond to them that

determines the outcome. While we may not be the direct cause of a situation we're in (a disease, a hurricane, an accident, the death of a loved one), we do get to decide how we ALLOW it to affect us. It's not about the load we are carrying, it's about how we choose to *carry* that load.

On the flip side, sometimes we are the direct CAUSE of why our lives aren't working. We weren't willing to put in the time, commitment, excellence, or energy necessary to have a flourishing relationship, career, or business venture. And when we get honest about being the CAUSE of our results, we can then get into action to change them.

If we take on the role of victim and blame our circumstances for why our lives aren't working, we can't do much to change the outcome, because blaming something outside of ourselves keeps the solution "out there," too. If we want to live powerful lives, we must get comfortable with creating our own reality and knowing that the solution to every problem lies within us.

If we want to move from Victim to Creator, we must take full, radical responsibility for the situation, and then go deeper and ask WHY we're being faced with this. Remember: Nothing happens TO us, it happens FOR us. Every moment in life is one that is presented for our highest growth. What lesson can be learned here? And if you find yourself saying, "Why does this always happen to me?" then the answer will inevitably be because you haven't learned the lesson that's there for you yet. I know it's hard to hear that all the seemingly "bad" things in life are actually directly tied to you, but if you truly listen to what I'm saying, you will actually find it quite liberating.

Once we take full responsibility for our lives, we get to step into our full power and decide how we would like to move forward. We get to create whatever outcome we want from a place of full accountability and integrity. Life will never stop being life; it will keep giving us a wide array of circumstances, both good and bad, and it is up to us to decide what we want to do with them.

YOUR MISSION: What have you been holding on to from the past that might be holding you back in the present moment?

_____

_____

_____

How are you responsible for this event, by either causing it or allowing it to affect you in a certain way?

_____

_____

_____

_____

What has this cost you? Have you missed out on fully showing up, experiencing love, feeling free, being happy, or trusting people?

_____

_____

_____

_____

_____

_____

Why did this happen FOR you? What lesson/breakthrough can you find in this breakdown or hurt?

_____

_____

_____

_____

_____

_____

REFLECTION: How did your initial feelings about a "negative" situation transform once you uncovered your role in it and its higher purpose or lesson for your life?

_____

_____

_____

_____

_____

_____

_____

Dear Human,

You know that thing you're going through right now?

Yes, I know it's "annoying," but I got that for you. (Yes, YOU.)

It's for your highest good.

There's a really amazing lesson in there, and once you figure

it out, you're gonna be so darn happy you did.

It's the beginning of a new way of looking at things.

One day, you'll look back on this "problem" and laugh.

Do you trust me? I sure hope so.

The Universe

#50WaysToYay

8. WHAT ARE YOU WAITING FOR?

As human beings, we're never guaranteed another day on this planet. While most of us will live long, happy lives, I have quite a few friends that never made it to their thirtieth birthday. They certainly weren't expecting to go so early, but one lesson I learned from them was that they lived their lives to the fullest: they dared greatly, they did what made their heart soar, and they told the people they cared most about how they felt.

While we all have varying levels of daily responsibilities to tend to, we can choose to approach our days with a sense of gratitude and passion. When I shifted into this way of living, everything shifted along with it. It wasn't that my circumstances drastically changed (I was still working in a career field that I wasn't particularly thrilled with), but I showed up differently. And within that small shift, I discovered joy that I had never experienced before, passion that had been lying dormant, and gratitude for the people and blessings I had in my life.

So don't let another day pass you by without choosing to feel ALIVE. Do those things that you've always wanted to do. Say those things that you've always wanted to say. Be the highest version of yourself TODAY, while you have the gift of LIFE. We're not promised another day, so do it now. If not now . . . when?

YOUR MISSION: What are three things you've been wanting to do, say, and be that you've been putting off for the "perfect" time?

DO: _____

SAY: _____

BE: _____

Pick ONE of those listed above and TAKE ACTION toward it today.

REFLECTION: Was your mission really as scary as you thought it would be? Knowing that you're capable of following through, what's next on your list to accomplish?

_____
_____
_____
_____

IF NOT *now,* THEN *when?*
IF NOT **YOU,** THEN *who?*

#50WaysToYay

Be unreasonable.

BE UNSTOPPABLE.

Be insanely committed.

#50WaysToYay

9. BE A PERSON OF PERSISTENCE

Nothing can get in the way of a committed person. No circumstances. No haters. No obstacle. No rejection. Being 100 percent committed to a vision means there is absolutely no room for excuses and only room for results. When we persist at something, we make a way out of no way and keep at it until we reach our desired destination. When we're insanely committed to our vision, the Universe paves a path for us, because we give it no other option.

To really drill this lesson home in my trainings, I use a simple yet powerful metaphor. Imagine that you've been dreaming of going on a particular road trip. You've planned for it, you've mapped out the way, you've dreamed about what the journey will look like, you've saved money for it and taken time off, and you can almost taste how sweet arriving at your final destination will be. The day has finally come. Bags packed and ready to go, you hit the road. You're cruising along and all of a sudden, about seventy miles along, you realize you have a flat tire. Do you get out, fix the flat, and get back to the trip of your dreams? Or do you get out, slash all the tires, burn the vehicle (and all of your stuff in it), and hitch a ride back into town? If you're a rational human being, chances are you'd fix the flat and get back to your trip of a lifetime. (If you chose the latter option, remind me to never lend you my car.) When it comes to our vision and dreams, MOST of us quit at the first sign of a challenge, slash the proverbial tires, burn the car, and walk away completely defeated before we even really got anywhere.

One of my mentors put this beautifully. Jim Rohn states that we must "do it UNTIL"—until we reach our desired outcome, until we hit that benchmark we're after, until we grasp what we've been wanting to hold. This level of unwavering persistence is what parents give their children when teaching them how to walk. They're not going to let the child stop walking because he fell a couple of times; they'll keep practicing with him UNTIL he walks. Period.

If we want to live extraordinary lives, we must consistently do whatever it takes—whether we feel like it or not. We must get excited about every roadblock we encounter, because we know that every obstacle is an opportunity to get better. We must be willing to push past our excuses and our "reasons" and get completely unreasonable with our thoughts and actions. We must be courageous enough to do what most people are unwilling to do, and persist when most people would break. Extraordinary people have an insane amount of hustle, are unstoppable in the face of no, and refuse to quit until they reach their destination.

YOUR MISSION:

What obstacle or roadblock in your relationship, your vision, or your goals are you currently facing?

_____

_____

_____

_____

What alternative route could you create to reach the destination you desire and persist no matter what?

_____

_____

_____

_____

REFLECTION: Looking back on your life, would you consider yourself a person of persistence? If you answered YES, what has being persistent created for you; how could you foster more of that? If you answered NO, in which areas of your life would you like to commit to being a person of persistence?

_____

_____

_____

_____

_____

_____

_____

_____

YOU

become

WHAT YOU

surround yourself

WITH.

#50WaysToYay

10. THE 40/40/20 RULE

Want to know how you're doing in this race of life? Look at who is around you, because you are likely the average of the five people that you spend the most time with. If they're moving slowly, chances are you are, too, because a pace has been set and you'll be only as fast as the fastest person on your team. But if you have someone on your team who is blazing past all limitations and has her sights set on breaking previous records, the entire team will pick up their own pace to try to keep up.

A great example of this is the story of Roger Bannister. For years, experts claimed that the human body was simply not capable of a 4-minute mile, that it was physically impossible to push the body to those extremes. Thousands of runners tried to break this barrier, going through intense training in their efforts to achieve the seemingly "impossible." In fact, in the 1940s the mile record was pushed all the way to 4:01, where it stood for nine years. Then, on May 6, 1954, everything changed when Roger Bannister finally broke the 4-minute mile, clocking in at 3 minutes and 59 seconds. After this new standard was set for what was possible, within that same year someone else ran a mile in less than 4 minutes. Now, sixty-plus years later, even strong high school runners can easily complete this distance in less than 4 minutes. What was once deemed impossible is now commonplace, all because of one man who challenged others to step up their game.

So what does this mean? We rise to what we see is possible. If the people you surround yourself with are playing at the same level or LOWER than where you're trying to play, you're never going to get any better. If you step up your game, and surround yourself with a team of people who are achieving more than you, you will inevitably rise to what you see is possible. So if you want to go pro, you have to spend less time with the amateurs and be courageous enough to learn from the best. Success leaves clues, and if we want a life of more happiness, abundance, connection, and fulfillment, we have to be willing to learn from the people who are thriving in these areas of life.

This brings me to the 40/40/20 Rule. When I began taking stock of the people I spent the most time with, it was no surprise that my life looked the way it looked. While I was having a blast being a social butterfly who knew everyone and was out every night, I certainly wasn't living up to my full potential. So I stepped up my game. I began spending 40 percent of my time hanging around people and reading books from those who were more successful than me in the areas of my life that I wanted to develop and improve. This kept my skills sharp and allowed me to grow exponentially. I also got strategic about finding people who were looking to create on the level that I wanted to create on (what I call my success circle) and spent 40 percent of my time with them. This allowed me to have a support team of people equally as committed to their visions whom I could bounce ideas off of and stay motivated with on a daily basis. Then I spent the remaining 20 percent of my time being a source of information and inspiration to others who were looking to learn and grow in areas that I had done well in. This allows me to stay in the practice of giving back, and it strengthens what I'm learning every time I share it.

The 40/40/20 Rule has truly expanded everything that I'm doing in life. It's created exponential growth, nonstop motivation and support, and built-in contribution. When we have a surplus of those traits in our lives, we have a surplus of happiness to tap into.

YOUR MISSION: On a scale of 1 to 10, what level would you say you're playing at in the overall game of life?

_____

What five people (who would challenge you to step up your game) could you spend 40 percent of your time learning from—in books, workshops, seminars, or just over coffee?

1. _____
2. _____
3. _____
4. _____
5. _____

What five peers could you spend 40 percent of your time with, keeping one another accountable, motivated, and inspired on the journey?

1. _____
2. _____
3. _____
4. _____
5. _____

How could you spend 20 percent of your time sharing what you've learned along the way?

1. _____
2. _____

REFLECTION: Which group of the 40/40/20 do you need to develop most? What will you do to develop it?

_____
_____
_____
_____
_____
_____
_____
_____

11. PRACTICE RANDOM ACTS OF AWESOME

There's nothing quite as exciting as a random act of awesome: when someone buys you a cup of coffee just because, when your partner surprises you with a night out at your favorite place, or when someone drops a compliment bomb on you that just explodes shards of awesomeness all over your day. A magical spark comes from these random acts, and if we want to create more happiness and joy in our lives, we get to be the catalyst of that spark whenever we choose.

Today, practice a random act of awesome. Look for ways to leave people feeling absolutely over the moon. Give a little extra awesome in every interaction you have, every project you complete, every step (or skip!) you take, and every word you speak. Awesomeness is truly addictive and leaves the world a little more magical because of it.

YOUR MISSION: Find ONE way today to practice a random act of awesome.

REFLECTION: How amazing did it feel for you to give that much love and excitement, randomly, to someone or something else? What did it do for you?

_____

_____

_____

_____

_____

_____

_____

_____

Find any excuse to practice random acts of AWESOME.

#50WaysToYay

12. BE INTERESTED, NOT JUST INTERESTING

Spend more time being interested and less time trying to be interesting.

It's crazy to think about how much energy I used to put into making sure I was "interesting" to my partner, my friends, my family, people I worked with, even strangers! I felt as if I always had to lead with my best stuff to ensure that everyone knew just how interesting I was. But I missed out on so much of the incredible life that was happening all around me because I was so caught up in what other people thought of ME.

My focus on trying to be interesting was really about not believing that what I was doing was ALREADY interesting, so I tried to prove it to myself by proving it to others. Being so caught up in the "do they find me impressive yet?" loop, I couldn't see past this anxiety into all of the amazing things that both I and the people around me were creating.

Since I became aware of my unconscious "self-involvement," I've curbed talking about what I'm up to, and have found so much joy in getting to know new and old friends alike. I traded the constant feeling of anxiety over what others would think for a childlike sense of wonder and excitement that stays with me wherever I go. It's mind-blowing how much I continue to learn about people I've known forever, and how incredible every single person truly is. Everyone has a story: the cabdriver, the barista at the coffee shop, the young mom in line next to you, your parents, and your beloved. What's even more awesome is how curious I became about the simple things in life, and how much that curiosity completely transformed my experiences from mundane and boring into moments of magic and awe.

When we assume that we know someone or something already, we are discounting the daily growth and evolution that happens along the journey; we expect the same old same and lose that magical feeling of NEWNESS that could be there if we just chose to acknowledge it. Life is all about relationships: our relationships with one another and our relationship with our surroundings. And for those who say they're lonely or bored: well, there are 7 BILLION people in the world and we have every opportunity to at least say hello and strike up a conversation with the twenty-plus people we come into contact with on a daily basis. There is an endless amount of wonder to behold in nature and in the Universe at large. It's amazing what happens when we step out of our own little Vortex of Self and start to genuinely get curious—all that stress and insecurity just melts away.

So if you want more joy and excitement in your life, don't be so definitive about people, nature, and things; be open and live in a constant state of curious wonder and exploration, and you'll find that there is always something waiting, ready to blow your mind.

YOUR MISSION: Today, when you encounter an "old" situation, show up with a newfound curiosity. If it's a person you're used to seeing all the time, ask new questions and dig a little deeper. Try to find out one thing about that person that you never knew before. If it's your surroundings, try to notice something that you've never noticed before; get curious about the world around you.

REFLECTION: What new things did you learn or discover about someone or your surroundings? What did this exercise open up for you?

_____

_____

_____

_____

_____

_____

_____

_____

Spend more time
BEING *interested*

AND LESS TIME

TRYING TO BE INTERESTING.

Find what you're good at,
AND THEN DO THAT.

#50WaysToYay

13. YOU'RE A GENIUS

Generally, as a society, we tend to think of "smarts" as a matter of intellect. However, I like to think that we all have a bit of genius in us. We are all exceptionally smart at something and have a unique aptitude for whatever that is in our lives. We may have a propensity for languages or a great deal of athletic ability; some of us are highly creative and can compose music or produce outstanding works of art; others may be crazy talented at people skills or are unbelievable parents. There are those who are researchers or explorers and those who can REALLY teach.

The trouble is, most of us aren't doing what we're exceptionally great at; we're on a hamster wheel doing a bunch of things that we're just mediocre at, never getting to experience a state of flow because we're operating at less than our potential. If we think of the truly great people in life—people such as Wolfgang Amadeus Mozart, Martin Luther King Jr., Michael Jordan, and Michael Jackson—we see people who have truly tapped into their Core Genius. Could you imagine if Mozart had been forced to be an accountant? Or if Martin Luther King had taken a job in sales? The world would've missed out on some pretty incredible gifts, and we don't want to let that happen with you.

Psychologist Abraham Maslow has said, "What human beings can be, they must be." There's an inherent need or impulse within each of us to become that which we are capable of becoming. And while I'm not saying we should all quit our jobs and focus 100 percent on our Core Genius, I am saying that it's a crime to not use the gifts that we've been given during our time on this earth. We each have an area of our lives in which we naturally excel and we must start honoring that, even if it's only in our free time. The more we operate from our Core Genius, the more we experience a state of effortlessness and flow; the more flow we experience, the more joyfully we participate in each and every day of life.

YOUR MISSION: What is one thing that you're exceptionally great at? What do you do with ease, grace, and a sense of bliss? (If you're not sure where your Core Genius may be, ask someone who knows you really well.)

_____

_____

How can you bring more of this into your daily life?

_____

_____

_____

REFLECTION: If you truly embraced your Core Genius and began to spend more time with it, what do you think it would be possible to create in life?

_____

_____

_____

_____

Focus on the vision,

AND YOU WON'T EVEN NOTICE

THE OBSTACLES.

#50WaysToYay

14. EYE ON THE PRIZE

In life, we get more of what we focus on.

During a six-month leadership program that I took, all of us students were faced with a particular challenge. We were to break an arrow in half by placing the pointed end of it on the soft part of our throats (just above our collarbone) and the end of the arrow against the wall (perpendicular to us). We were told to use our legs for momentum, tense up our upper body by clenching our fists, and then focus on trying to plow through the wall with our nose. Needless to say, all twenty of the students, including myself, were a little apprehensive. I was the third person to go and I did exactly as I was instructed: used my legs for momentum, tensed up my upper body, and thrust my nose toward the wall with everything I had.

Good news . . . I'm still alive! The arrow split in half and my skin barely had a mark on it. Meanwhile, a few other students went and stopped about 10 percent of the way in because the sensation of the tip of the arrow on their throat triggered a fear response. Others made it only halfway to the wall—barely bending the arrow, let alone breaking it—before they stopped. How was this possible? After talking with my classmates, both those who broke the arrow and those who didn't, I realized that it all came down to focus. It's not that those of us that broke the arrow are secret superheroes and turned on our super strength to break the arrow (although if I was, I'd like to be one who wears a unicorn horn . . . just for the record), it was simply because we were following directions.

I did exactly as I was instructed: I focused on breaking through the wall with my nose. With my attention concentrated on the wall, I thought, "Wall, wall, wall," and my actions were confident and strong because there was nothing scary to me about moving toward the wall. The key here is that the thought of the arrow wasn't even a part of my experience. The students who had a more difficult time with the exercise were totally focused on the arrow: "What if the arrow pierces my throat? What if the arrow won't break? Sharp objects scare me. Why the heck are we breaking an arrow with our throats anyway?"

What this exercise showed me was that when we focus on the vision and set a strong intention to get there (breaking through the wall with our nose), our attention follows suit (wall) and our actions move us toward bringing that vision into reality (nose toward wall, arrow subsequently breaks). However, if we've set the intention we desire (breaking the wall with our nose) *but* we keep our vision focused on the obstacle (the arrow), our attention focuses all of our energy on the obstacle (the arrow) and our actions become laced with fear, doubt, and uncertainty, and we inevitably get caught up in the obstacle.

So what are you primarily focused on? Take a moment and reflect on where you consistently place your attention. All of the people and circumstances that we attract are directly related to where we invest our attention. It's all well and good to *intend* to experience a beautiful, joy-filled life, but if that intention is out of alignment with our attention (and we're focusing on fear and limitation), then we'll only get more of what we're placing our focus on. So be honest: are you focused on the arrow—on what's not working, on the lack and limitations you're experiencing, on the fear that comes up, or on what is seemingly standing in your way? Or are you focused on breaking through the wall—on a greater vision; on something that is so important to you that you will let nothing stand in your way?

The fastest way to change how we feel about anything in life is to change what we're giving our attention to, because whatever we focus on, we ultimately get more of. So if we want to overcome challenges with confidence and ease, we must create a powerful vision for our lives that we can set our sights on. When we keep our eye on the prize and align our attention with our intention, we're so incredibly focused on that vision that we barely see the many obstacles in our way.

YOUR MISSION: What powerful intention or vision can you establish for yourself in each area of your life? What will you have to focus on in order to keep your eye on the prize?

Relationships:
(Intention) _____
(Attention) _____

Career:
(Intention) _____
(Attention) _____

Finances:
(Intention) _____
(Attention) _____

Health:
(Intention) _____
(Attention) _____

REFLECTION: Understanding that what we put our attention on we get more of, what negative situations or circumstances can you now take responsibility for? What was your attention focused on that created this?

_____

_____

_____

_____

_____

_____

_____

15. CHANGE YOUR LENS

Albert Einstein said that we can't solve a problem with the same level of consciousness that created it, and I couldn't agree more. If you're looking for a solution to any problem, the answer lies outside of your current understanding of what you know to be possible. If we change the lens we're looking through, we instantly expand our perspective.

A great area to apply this lesson is with relationships, whether it's one with our family, our friends, our coworkers, or our romantic partner. When a disagreement arises, we often jump straight into how that person doesn't understand US. We are viewing the issue through a narrow lens called ME and thus spend our time arguing and defending our position on why we're right and the other person is wrong. All we can see is how the situation affects US, because that's all that the limited lens of ME can focus on. The other party involved is often doing the exact same thing, fighting for their position and standing firm in their own righteousness. What if, in the thick of an argument, you could remove the lens called ME and try on the lens called THEM? Then you could see how others are feeling and have more empathy for their needs and what they're experiencing. While you're at it, you could put on the objective lens called WE and see the situation simply as it is, without taking anything personally: person A wants this and person B wants that; now, how do we come to a consensus that works? Take that up a notch and try on the widest lens called LOVE. This lens can see only love and will do whatever it takes to bring that love into focus. This is the lens that begs to ask: how can I BE love in this moment?

Until we are willing to remove our narrow personal lens called ME, we will always see the world through our skewed viewpoint. If we want to create more harmony in our lives and in the world at large, we must be willing to switch out our lens and see things from various perspectives.

YOUR MISSION: Think of a current or past situation that still feels unresolved in which you may be holding on to some resentment, hurt, or anger. Change your lens from your personal focus to others with a more objective, wider focus. How might the other person feel about the situation and your involvement in it? What is he or she waiting on from you? If you had to take full responsibility for the situation, without any blame whatsoever falling on the other party, what would that look like? How could you BE love?

_____

_____

_____

_____

_____

_____

_____

_____

REFLECTION: How did changing your lens change your perspective about this situation?

_____

_____

_____

_____

_____

_____

_____

_____

What action will you take now?

_____

_____

_____

_____

When searching
for CLARITY,
we must widen our
PERSPECTIVE.

#50WaysToYay

A high-quality life

HAS MUCH MORE TO DO WITH

what we remove from it

THAN WITH WHAT WE ADD TO IT.

#50WaysToYay

16. SIMPLIFY

A high-quality life has much more to do with what we remove from it than with what we add to it. The acquisition of more stuff reminds us that where we are and what we have is not quite enough yet, leaving us feeling empty and deficient. On the contrary, the actions of giving things away, paring down our stuff, and being grateful for what we already have remind us that not only do we have more than enough, but we actually have abundance in our lives; and acting from a place of abundance attracts more abundance.

This is one of my favorite lessons. Maybe it's because I'm a Virgo and I like to organize; or maybe it's because it really works. Every time I'm getting ready for new opportunities or deeper clarity in my life (whether it's launching a new program or taking my spiritual work to a new level), I clear out and organize an area of my home. I'll go through my things, pare down and donate as much as possible in order to create space for magic to happen. Without fail, within mere days of this physical and energetic clearing, a new opportunity will pop into my world. This also works wonders whenever I'm feeling stagnant or creatively blocked. Remember, it's impossible for us to bring in new opportunities, people, clarity, ideas, or circumstances if our lives are already at capacity and splitting at the seams.

I learned this very practical tool through ten years of travel with my nonprofit E.P.I.C., to Tanzania, Africa. My partner and

I dedicate our time in Tanzania to bringing clean, sustainable water to rural communities in need. Most of these villages lack more than just potable water; they lack electricity, plumbing, proper washrooms, and shelter. But there is something that always seems to be overflowing in the communities we work in: a spirit of love, happiness, community, and LIFE. The Tanzanians we work with rarely have more than one or two outfits to their name, yet they seem exponentially happier than most people I know in the developed world. They own only what they truly need, and are incredibly grateful for what they do have. This attitude of gratitude is prevalent in every home we visit, and in my dealings with them I recognize what true abundance looks like. While they don't have some of the most basic needs of human beings, they feel that they have abundance because they're grateful for what they do have: family, love, nature, culture, and community. They certainly don't have the stuff most of us would paste on our vision boards, like fancy cars and homes, but they have the stuff that our souls call out for.

Now, I'm not suggesting we should all give up our possessions and move out to the wilderness (though there is nothing wrong with that); rather, I'm presenting the option that we find a new way to relate to our lives of modern conveniences and endless options. I'm challenging us to remove the clutter and make room for what is truly important in life. When we practice the art of simplicity, we realize that there are so many things to be truly grateful for; and a grateful spirit calls forth an inner happiness that can never be taken away.

YOUR MISSION: Find one area of your home that you can clean, clear out, and get rid of any excess that you don't need or use. The area can be as small as a drawer or as large as an entire room. Your mission is to create space that will leave proverbial "room" for a new sense of clarity, opportunity, ideas, or a new person to come into your life.

REFLECTION: How does it feel to get rid of the excess clutter and stuff? Did it create more lightness within you? Do you have a deeper awareness of how fortunate you truly are? What might be the next location to pare down and clear out?

_____

_____

_____

_____

_____

_____

_____

_____

Get comfortable with the DISCOMFORT ZONE.

#50WaysToYay

17. THE ONE THING YOU CAN COUNT ON

If you're standing still, doing the same old thing, and nothing's changed lately, you're actually going BACKWARD. The world is consistently moving FORWARD, forever evolving and changing, and it's not waiting for you to catch up. That is the ONE thing we can know for sure: things will always change.

The Buddhists call this transient state of all things impermanence. All things of the world are in a constant state of flux, and we can count on everything as we know it to shift and change with time.

This is a hard one for a lot of us to grasp, as human beings are mostly creatures of comfort. We tend to like what we like, and we would prefer to never experience the feelings of loss that inevitably come with change. But change truly is unavoidable. We will age. Our relationships will change. We'll have times of abundance and times of financial drought. Just as nature has its seasons, we will go through seasons of life wrought with inevitable change. But if we can be flexible with life, unattached to the notion of things staying the same, we can create a baseline of joy that expects, welcomes, and dances with the change that is bound to come. So don't just get comfortable with change, seek new ways to constantly evolve who you are and what you're working on. There's always a deeper level to dive into or a bigger court to play on.

YOUR MISSION: Are you someone who tends to embrace change or do you cringe at the notion of uncertainty?

_____

_____

What area of your life can you focus on evolving and taking to the next level?

_____

_____

_____

_____

REFLECTION: Why do you think you've been avoiding change in this particular area? What does shifting out of your comfort zone bring up for you?

_____

_____

_____

_____

_____

_____

_____

18. BE YOU . . . EVERYONE ELSE IS ALREADY TAKEN

The YOU that you are is completely unique. Think about it: there are seven BILLION people in the world, and only ONE just like you. Whoa . . . pretty cool, huh? Just as we all have our own unique fingerprint, I firmly believe that we also have our own unique *soul* fingerprint.

Osho, one of my favorite mystics, states this lesson beautifully: "Each person is born with a unique individuality, and each person has a destiny of his or her own. Imitation is a crime, it is criminal. If you try to become a Buddha, you may look like Buddha, you may walk like him, you may talk like him, but you will miss. You will miss all that life was ready to deliver to you. Buddha happens only once. It is not in the nature of things to repeat. Existence is so creative that it never repeats anything. You cannot find another human being in the present, in the past, or in the future who is going to resemble you exactly. It has never happened. The human being is not a mechanism like Ford cars on an assembly line. Never imitate anybody."

When we compare ourselves to others, we disown our true essence because we think that our light will shine brighter if only we had what THEY have; meanwhile, we ignore the incredible, full expression of light that we already are. When we're in a state of comparison, we hide who we really are from the world because we don't think that we're enough, inevitably robbing the world of the unique gift that only we can offer. When we quit trying to live a life that was meant for someone else, we allow what is already inside of us to shine through; and the Universe paves a path for our distinct purpose to unfold.

Pablo Picasso once said, "The meaning of life is to find your gift. The purpose of life is to give it away," and he hit the nail on the head. You were born with a unique combination of things that no one else was born with, and when you allow yourself to tap into that gift, you allow that gift to guide your life. True happiness is about embracing all of who you are and letting that full expression of your light shine out into the world, with a deep knowing and trust that who you are is exactly who you need to be.

NOBODY IS GOING TO ACCEPT YOU UNTIL YOU ACCEPT YOURSELF

Every time we feel rejected, it means we're waiting for someone else's approval or acceptance to validate who we are. If we base our sense of worth on external circumstances or the opinion of others, our self-confidence will always be in limbo. We need to be loyal to ourselves. We need to love ourselves and accept who we are, flaws and all. From there, we can evolve and grow from a place of love and self-respect.

When we fully accept and embrace who we are, we stop looking to the outside world to convince us that we're worthy, because we intrinsically know that we already are; we stop wasting our energy on trying to prove that we're good enough, talented enough, and good-looking enough. When we stop wasting our time trying to impress others, we free up energy to cultivate the incredible being that we are. After all, what good is it to have the approval of the world if we've completely lost who we are in the process?

This lesson, as crazy as it sounds, saved my life. For years I based my value and worthiness on the good opinion of others, and as I inevitably rose and fell in their estimation, my confidence and sense of worth would rise and fall, as well. This endless cycle of searching for validation left me feeling desperately unhappy and obsessed with achievement. I thought that if I could achieve enough, the world would finally deem me worthy (as if that was even possible).

This led me to complete burnout and exhaustion. I was doing, doing, doing, because I didn't feel worthy enough to simply BE. When I finally ran out of steam and my body physically shut down on me—I contracted a crazy kidney infection that had me bedridden for weeks—I saw the insidious pattern that I had created and began to truly work on being enough without having to prove myself to anybody. I had to learn to accept all of who I was, even though some of it wasn't so pretty. I had to learn to forgive myself and embrace the fact that I made some not-so-wise decisions that I ultimately found gratitude for because they brought me to the person I am today. I began focusing on the beautiful qualities that I possessed and led with those qualities in my interactions with others. I began to take care of ME and nurture the desires of my soul. That ultimately changed the way I viewed and loved myself. I began to truly see the gift that I was, and I started embracing that gift and letting it shine. When I genuinely began to see, acknowledge, embrace, and *own* how amazing and worthy I was, other people began to see the same thing and treat me accordingly. It wasn't until I sincerely accepted myself that others could accept me.

When we make it our mission to be ourselves fully, without comparing ourselves to other people, we allow our unique soul fingerprint to be expressed in the world. The truth is, the world needs you to be YOU so the picture of the world makes sense. We're all little puzzle pieces, and it's just plain old annoying when a piece is missing.

YOUR MISSION: What are three things about you that make you unique?

1. _____
2. _____
3. _____

Choose ONE of those things and celebrate it or show it off today.

REFLECTION: How does it feel to celebrate your unique qualities? How can you do this more often?

_____
_____
_____
_____
_____
_____
_____
_____

YOU'RE AN
essential piece
OF THIS PUZZLE CALLED LIFE.

WITHOUT THE
full expression of you,
THE PICTURE JUST DOESN'T

MAKE SENSE.

#50WaysToYay

It's not what you
DO ONCE THAT
MATTERS,
it's what you
DO DAY IN AND DAY OUT
that makes the difference.

19. DAILY DEPOSITS

We'll never be able to change our lives until we are willing to change our habits. It's not what we do ONCE that makes us broke, out of shape, or has our relationship fall apart; conversely, it's not the onetime action that makes us wealthy, a fitness god, or creates an incredible relationship. It's what we do *daily* that ultimately determines our destiny.

Feeding our "life account" with healthy food and exercise, nurturing our relationships with love and appreciation, and paying ourselves first are what I like to call Daily Deposits. These daily life-giving actions create a surplus in our accounts and lead to an incredibly fulfilling life. These are the small but significant decisions that, if done consistently, will change our lives for the better and lead to some amazing results.

However, if we're constantly in a state of "withdrawal" on our life account (eating an excessive amount of junk, watching too much TV, not working out, not tending to our relationships, spending more than we make, not sleeping enough, or complaining all the time), these actions will lead to a growing *negative* balance. We'll be overdrawn and feel exhausted, miserable, and out of shape because we failed to make small decisions that could have led to a different outcome.

Most people claim that it is a lack of discipline that keeps their life accounts in the negative; but what they don't see is that they are simply disciplined in bad habits; they have created the discipline of watching TV every night or the discipline of eating processed foods. They are disciplined to be on their phones while out on a date, and disciplined not to work out. It's not a matter of discipline, just a matter of *what* we're disciplined to do.

So how is your account looking? Are there areas where you're depositing like crazy and other areas where you're overdrawn? Is your account flourishing, at break-even, or in the red? What are your daily disciplines looking like? Take stock of where you are today and start changing up the daily habits that don't serve you anymore. Let's start filling the proverbial piggy bank and it just might add up to something pretty darn incredible.

YOUR MISSION:

What daily disciplines or habits of yours have added value to your life account?

1. _____
2. _____
3. _____

What daily disciplines or habits of yours have withdrawn value from your life account?

1. _____
2. _____
3. _____

What small change can you make today that will bring you closer to where you want to be? It could be saving five dollars, not eating any more doughnuts, having a salad for lunch instead of a hamburger, expressing gratitude toward your loved ones, or going for a walk on your break.

_____

_____

REFLECTION: How did it feel to do something for yourself that accelerated your growth and brought you one step closer to where you want to be?

_____

_____

_____

_____

_____

_____

_____

_____

Add gratitude

FOR INSTANT HAPPINESS.

#50WaysToYay

20. JUST ADD GRATITUDE!

I hear a lot of people say, "I JUST want to be happy." So, what's the secret to finding happiness?

Well, the first thing to know is that happiness doesn't exist somewhere out there; it's an inside job. Happiness is created by a moment-to-moment choice to be grateful. And when we make that choice over and over again, we create a habit of happiness. The more we focus on what we're grateful for, the more we train our brain to focus on and hunt for more opportunities to be grateful.

Conversely, negativity is a choice as well, one that when made over and over again can become a habit. The more we focus on what's not working in our lives, by complaining, worrying, and always finding the bad in every situation, the more we train our brains to seek out and bring negativity to the forefront.

Gratitude is key to uncovering instant happiness. It's simply impossible to feel stressed-out, anxious, fearful, or depressed when we're in a state of pure gratitude. And while the situations of our lives may not be exactly what we want, we can always find something to be grateful for, even if it's as simple as being grateful for being alive to experience whatever it is that we may be going through.

If you want more *YAY!* in your life, you must consistently choose to practice gratitude in order to train your brain to find more of it. Gratitude is one of the quickest paths to real happiness and peace in life, and it's always just a choice away.

YOUR MISSION: What are three things that you are grateful for today?

1. _____
2. _____
3. _____

Today, notice when emotions of fear come up. Choose gratitude in those moments to reframe your focus.

REFLECTION: Were you able to keep up the practice of gratitude throughout the day? How did it feel to reframe a potentially negative situation?

_____
_____
_____
_____
_____
_____
_____
_____

Your body
IS YOUR VEHICLE
TO EXPLORE LIFE IN—
take good care of it.

#50WaysToYay

21. MAINTENANCE REQUIRED

If you're reading this, your heart is beating and your breath is flowing. Congratulations . . . you've made it another day! Unfortunately, most of us don't appreciate our health while we have it; we wish and pray for it to come back only when we suddenly come down with an illness. But why wait for disaster to strike? Why not appreciate and honor your body while it's working?

Your health is everything; it's a part of what TRUE wealth really is. The sad truth is, most of us take better care of our cars, shoes, or houses than we do the physical home that our spirit resides in. If we want to experience our full capacity for joy in life, we need to first have a body that feels good.

I could write an entire book on this topic because I'm incredibly passionate about it, and there are a ton of fantastic resources out there already if you really want to take your health up a notch—but we all have an understanding of the basics: eat tons of healthy, chemical-free fruits and vegetables, drink plenty of water throughout the day, move your body daily, reduce stress with meditation, and ensure you are getting the rest your body needs. Do your best to avoid processed foods and sugary drinks, be aware of the chemicals in your foods and beauty products that your body is soaking up, and limit your alcohol intake. I get that it may be hard to switch up some of your habits, but this is the only body you've got. Invest in loving it now, and it will pay off in the long run.

Don't wait until it's too late. Your body is your temple and your only vehicle for exploring life; take great care of it.

YOUR MISSION: Take this moment and honor your amazing machine of a body that has brought you to another day of life. Put your hand over your heart, feel its rhythm, and thank it for its tireless work. Take a deep breath in, fill your lungs with all of that oxygen, and release it with gratitude, knowing that you get to experience another magical day on planet Earth.

What is one new habit you can start today that will nourish a healthy, happy body moving forward?

_____

_____

Why is it important that you commit to this new habit?

_____

_____

_____

REFLECTION: With this awareness of the gift of health, how were your choices different today? How did that feel?

_____

_____

_____

_____

_____

22. PRACTICE COMPASSION

In every interaction, be gentle with one another because we're all learning something new. We're all dealing with our lives in our own particular way; and we each have a unique story and history that colors who we show up as. Be compassionate and try to meet people where they are. Resist the urge to judge anyone because we're all in a process of learning and growing.

This sense of compassion and understanding of others has been instrumental in creating a lasting baseline of joy in my life. In the past, when I would get into disagreements, I would take things personally. I would see the other person's argument as an attack on who I was, and then go into defensiveness almost immediately. As you can imagine, that never ended well. However, as I continue to apply this lesson of compassion in my life, I am able to be calmer and more rational, and lead from a place of love rather than defense. I see that both the other person and I are acting out of our wounds, and then I can begin to respond from a more grounded and loving place.

When we can enter into situations with the understanding that people who are hurting are usually the ones who hurt others, we see that it is most often nothing personal. Once we realize this, we can behave more objectively. We can choose to support and help heal the root cause of their pain, or we can simply have compassion for their pain and choose not to participate in the exchange. While this may sound simple, it's one of the hardest things to do. If we can continuously choose to see humanity from the understanding that we're all in a learning process, it will literally shift how we interact in the world. Anger and resentment won't be so quick to take over, and we'll have a deeper sense of peace and joy that comes from this place of compassion.

A great way to stay present to this lesson while in a difficult interaction is to imagine the other person as a three-year-old child whom you love: someone who doesn't know any better, someone who is hurting, who is experiencing his or her own pain or struggle, but doesn't have the wherewithal to handle it properly. Then we can choose to show up and help HEAL the situation with love (rather than trying to argue with a three-year-old).

YOUR MISSION:
Today, be gentle with everyone. Look at them with eyes of understanding and compassion. Recognize that we are all on our own journey and at different points on the path.

REFLECTION: How did it feel to give people the benefit of the doubt, to be a little easier on everyone, and recognize we're all in a process of growth and healing?

_____

_____

_____

_____

_____

BE GENTLE WITH EACH OTHER;

we're all learning something new.

#50WaysToYay

23. CHILD'S EYES

As children, we are open to learning and exploring the magic that is life. We are curious, loving, free, and fully self-expressed, and quick to forget any hurt that comes upon us. As adults, we tend to get a bit jaded, complacent, and way too comfortable in our routines, forgetting to see the world as an endless source of wonder. We hold on to hurt, we become bitter with our experiences, and we close ourselves off from new ideas and new people. The open, free, and forgiving spirit of children IS OUR TRUE NATURE, but somewhere along the journey into adulthood we've allowed ourselves to forget this.

Age has many beautiful gifts, but a few that I could live without are pride, resentment, and the know-it-all mentality that seem to grow bigger with every passing year that brings us deeper into adulthood. You see, I used to be a total cynic. I used to turn my nose up to magic and serendipity, to faith and to hope. I used to think that love always had an expiration date, and that everyone always has an ulterior motive. People would tell me about their experiences of the "state of flow" and how everything is "as it's meant to be," and I would laugh to myself about how the fall from their cloud would feel when they hit the ground. What's worse, I used to take pride in my cynicism, seeing myself as one of the "realistic" ones, until that cynicism eventually resulted in a miserable life.

I distinctly remember the crisp September Saturday morning that shifted everything for me. I was sitting on a bench in New York City's Central Park, watching hundreds of people pass by. I saw many lifeless adult faces—people who seemed tired and worn-out, with no spark or spunk left. One by one they walked by—rigid bodies, shoulders slumped, mad at the world because it was "in their way." They all seemed in a hurry to get somewhere, but didn't seem too happy about wherever they were going. I watched and wondered what they were thinking and how they must view the world; I then wondered if that's how *I* looked to others. Often I would catch myself being irritated by the smallest things, always in such a frantic hurry to get somewhere. I would be mad at the people in my way and would end every day feeling completely exhausted.

While I was thinking this, a small child, about four or five years old, came running up to the bench that I was sitting on; his mom was by his side, smiling at him and me. Full of life, he was exuberant and endlessly curious. He instantly said hello to me and began asking me a million questions. He proceeded to show me what he knew about leaves and trees and to tell me about his squirrel friend he always sees near the very bench we were on. As he ran off to dance in the fall air (and search for his squirrel friend), his mom and I talked about the wonders of children, how pure and free they are. Children operate from a place of innocence where they're completely open to the mystery of life, where they feel free to express who they are, regardless of who's watching. It was that day that I decided that I would choose to see the world through a child's eyes; that I would throw away my cynicism and regain that incredible spark, freedom, and joy that I came into the world with.

ALEXI PANOS

Now I dance in the magic of life daily. I see serendipity all around me because I CHOOSE to see it. I see that love is everything and that I am that same love . . . eternally. I choose my experiences based on how my soul feels, and my endless curiosity brings me an endless supply of joy. When I was a cynic, my world felt heavy. My smile was drawn on to match what society would accept as happy, and my laughter never truly came from my gut. I used to be a cynic, and my wariness created space and separateness that kept validating my "reasons" for distrust. Now I smile so hard my face hurts, I laugh until I cry, and I hug people as if I haven't seen them in years. Life is filled with so many incredible people, places, and things to experience. There is an endless amount of magic; we just need to be willing to see it.

YOUR MISSION: Today, see the world through the eyes of the four-year-old you. Be curious. Laugh at the simple things. Smile at a stranger. Ask more questions. Express how you truly feel. Feel the freedom of wonder.

REFLECTION: How did it feel to see your day differently? How might you bring more of this explorative curiosity into each and every day?

_____

_____

_____

_____

_____

_____

_____

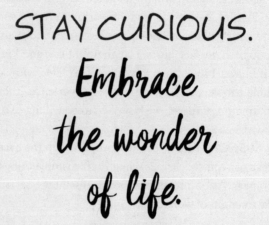

STAY CURIOUS.
Embrace
the wonder
of life.

#50WaysToYay

24. TAKE BACK YOUR TIME

You know that excuse you always use, "There's just not enough time"? Well, it actually doesn't work. As much as we don't want to admit it, we all have the same amount of time in a day: twenty-four hours. All of the people who have accomplished extraordinary feats, all of the "wizards" of productivity . . . well, we all have the same amount of time that they have.

We must understand that busyness does not necessarily equal productivity, and in order to accomplish anything in life, we must prioritize. What we put at the top of our list determines how we spend our time and how much value we get out of each and every day. The truth is, most of us are unconscious about how we *truly* spend our time, prioritizing things that we say don't really matter to us. We waste our extra time watching TV, complaining, or sleeping our lives away. We mindlessly scroll through social media and spend hours talking on the phone, and we don't make good use of our time traveling to and from work. We do so much in a day, yet wonder where all of our time went. Once we get honest about how we're actually spending our days, we can begin to prioritize what's most important to us, and start taking back our time.

When I was making the transition from my full-time career as a model and TV host into my current business, I knew I had to make some shifts in how I was spending my time. I declined countless invitations to enticing events and opportunities. I cut off the cable and strictly limited my time on the phone and the Internet. I said no to anything that didn't bring me closer to my vision, because I was saying yes to living the life that I dreamed of. I changed my habits, and I was able to build my dream business between the hours of six p.m. and one a.m. I would work full, busy days at my job, all while utilizing my breaks and commute time to study and build out my marketing materials. Then as soon as I arrived home, I would hit the ground running. I knew that I *had* to begin living my passion and used any spare time I could create in order to make my dreams a reality. When I got serious about my priorities, it was as if time just opened up for me.

So how will you choose to use your gift of twenty-four hours? What will you do differently today that will shape the rest of your life? What time wasters could you scale back on to create more minutes in your day for things you say you want to do?

YOUR MISSION: If you created more time, what would you choose to do with it?

_____

_____

_____

_____

What are some time wasters in your life (TV, gossip, worry, complaining, oversleeping)? How much time do you estimate you spend on each one?

Time waster: _____
Time spent: _____

Time waster: _____
Time spent: _____

Time waster: _____
Time spent: _____

Circle ONE time waster you can cut out TODAY to create space for something you truly want.

REFLECTION: Knowing that it's counterproductive to use the excuse "There's just not enough time," how do you plan on continuing to create more space in your day for doing what makes you happy?

_____
_____
_____
_____

WE ALL HAVE

THE SAME

twenty-four hours

IN A DAY.

How will you use yours?

#50WaysToYay

25. DATE YOURSELF

Whether you're in a relationship or not, it's critical for you to date yourself. Most people are looking for their "other half," trying to find someone else to help them feel more whole. But no other person can complete you; only YOU can complete yourself. When we date ourselves, we are nurturing the wholeness that we are so that we can show up powerfully in all of our relationships.

I like to think of relationships as two circles. When one circle is in a relationship with another circle, the overlap is pure magic. If the circles happen to separate (even if only for a weekend!), there isn't this crazy feeling of loss, because each was a circle in and of itself to begin with. However, if a semicircle is looking to feel whole (and doesn't want to do the work to complete itself), it will often attract another semicircle. Two semicircles become ONE circle, feeling momentarily whole, each half banking on the hope that the other will make up for its shortcomings. This is a disastrous recipe for codependency. Each semicircle will be relying on the other to complete it and *make it* happy, never realizing that it's the job of each semicircle to complete itself.

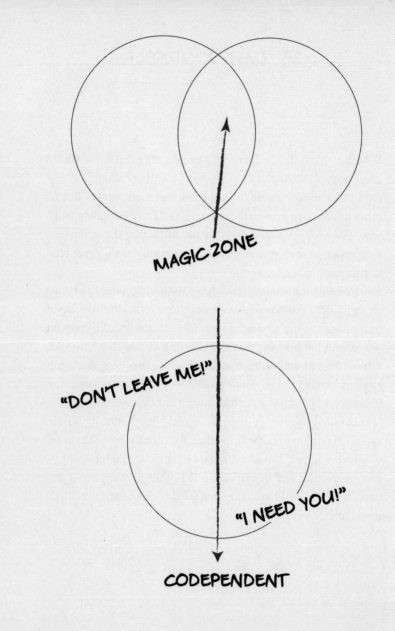

So if you don't want to enter the dreaded Codependent Zone in your current or future relationships, you have to begin nurturing that circle of yours with personal growth, self-awareness, and deepening your experience of what you love to do. Only when we are willing to be complete and enough on our own can we truly attract and maintain a healthy relationship.

YOUR MISSION: Create your DATE LIST. What are ten things you absolutely LOVE to do that you can enjoy by yourself? We're talking about those things that just make you feel all warm and fuzzy inside. Maybe it's lighting candles, playing eighties love songs, and splashing around in the bath? Or maybe it's putting your onesie on and watching the entire *Rocky* series. For me, going on a hike or sipping tea while strolling the aisles of a bookstore is my idea of a good time. Whatever it is, treat yourself at least once a week to a date with YOU. Take yourself out on the town or have a romantic evening in; whatever you love to do, do it. Don't wait for someone else to nurture you; you have yourself for that.

1. _____
2. _____
3. _____
4. _____
5. _____
6. _____
7. _____
8. _____
9. _____
10. _____

When, this week, are you going to take yourself out on **your first date?** _____ at _____ am/pm.

What time and day could you commit to every week, for an hour or two, for a personal date?

Every _____(day of the week)

At _____(time of day)

REFLECTION: Knowing that you have a list of ten things that light you up, how do you now feel about boredom or loneliness?

_____

_____

_____

_____

_____

_____

_____

_____

No one can
LOVE
you like you can.

#50WaysToYay

DISCONNECT TO

reconnect.

#50WaysToYay

26. UNPLUG

What on earth did we do before television, smartphones, the Internet, and video games? Drawing a blank?

In today's busy world, we find it hard not to get trapped by the lure of technology. In fact, the question is: Are we running *it* or or is it running *us*? Most of us spend the majority of our time at work on some form of electronic device, and then are quick to check our cell phones at the first free moment we can find. Technology certainly makes our lives a whole lot easier and more entertaining, but so much beauty also exists in the natural world around us. Many incredible things happen when we're out experiencing people, places, and nature; so let's give our weary eyes a break from the screen and do a little unplugging. Reconnect with the outdoors and let nature teach her lessons. Grab coffee with a friend instead of just texting back and forth for hours. Leave your phone at home and go out and create a new adventure that's worthy of a post when you get back.

Set some boundaries with technology so it doesn't take over your life. Give yourself a chance to disconnect from all devices in order to reconnect to the life unfolding before you. Your computer, tablet, and phone will be right where you left them when you get back . . . just make sure you lock your doors.

YOUR MISSION: Go without a device of any sort (cell phone, tablet, computer, e-reader, TV, iPod, stereo, etc.) for at least two hours. If you can make it that long, challenge yourself to go even longer. Be sure to eliminate all electronics while you're in the presence of friends or a loved one. Get connected to life around you.

REFLECTION: How did it feel to disconnect for a couple of hours? Was it frustrating or did you enjoy it? How were you able to reconnect in other ways without any reliance on a device, and what did you notice?

_____

_____

_____

_____

_____

_____

_____

Going forward, what boundaries can you set with technology? (Some examples are: ban technology from the bedroom or at the dinner table; check email once in the morning and once in the evening; limit the time you watch television.)

_____

_____

_____

_____

Growth

IS THE KEY TO

vitality.

#50WaysToYay

27. LEARN SOMETHING NEW

Lou Holtz, a former American football player, coach, and author, said, "In this world you're either growing or you're dying, so get in motion and grow." Learning something new energizes us and nurtures a sense of humility and curiosity. It leaves us in a constant state of wonder.

I was blessed to be born into a family where learning was fun. My "reward" as a kid was a trip to the library to pick out any book of my choosing, and our days playing outside with our parents were spent learning about the environment we were playing in. This is one gift that I'm eternally grateful for, because it's opened up so many beautiful doors for me in life.

As an adult I got bogged down and busy with life, and I realized I felt stuck and stagnant. I eventually attributed the complacency I was experiencing with my failure to continue to learn and grow. Because I was so caught up in my busyness, I wasn't reading like I used to, I wasn't taking any classes or learning any new skills, and I wasn't doing very much growing. When I remembered the joy that came with growth, I began to set up daily habits of reading and signed up for some classes that I was interested in. Almost instantly my mood began to shift as I learned more about the world and ultimately myself.

This lesson was drilled home for me when I read the *Tao*

Te Ching, a profound philosophical work written by Lao Tzu around 500 BC. In verse 76 of this ancient Chinese text, Lao Tzu likens us humans to plants. If we liken ourselves to a plant, then when we're not growing, we're in the process of dying. Without growth, we eventually become stiff and rigid in our ways. We begin to dull and wilt, losing our color and our vibrancy. We lose all capacity to produce fruit (our gifts) for the world, because we can barely keep ourselves upright. Eventually we dry up and no longer have much to offer. But if we are constantly feeding our souls, growing and learning something new each day, we remain supple and flexible. We soften with the humility that there is always more to learn. We enrich ourselves so that we may enjoy a richer existence and share our gifts with others. When we're committed to growth, we are essentially committed to our vitality.

So challenge yourself to learn something new every single day. Open up a book for ten minutes. Read an interesting article. Listen to a podcast. Take someone you respect out for coffee and learn about a skill set she might have. However you digest it, take in some new information and expand yourself. It's a constant reminder that we don't know everything and there's always something new to discover. Stay curious, my friends.

YOUR MISSION: Today is about stretching yourself. Learn ONE new skill, insight, quote, fact, or recipe. Take in something that expands your current level of consciousness and renews your sense of wonder and vitality.

REFLECTION: What did you learn today? What habit can you add into your daily routine to ensure you're always learning something new?

_____

_____

_____

_____

28. THE VALUE OF VULNERABILITY

If you know me, or know of my work, you'll likely be privy to the notion that I'm a recovering perfectionist. Perfectionism has plagued me for most of my life and I attached my value to how together or perfect I appeared. If others seemed to think my life was working, I would feel a sense of completeness and worthiness. I felt that if I had enough things going right, then the world wouldn't be able to tell that deep down I felt that I didn't quite measure up.

I used my seemingly perfect front like a brick wall: it hid the soft, messy, vulnerable parts of me from the world. While this ploy worked wonders for blocking judgments or criticism, it also kept all the goodness out. It prevented me from developing deep intimacy in my friendships and relationships, and it shielded me from feeling true joy and happiness. I felt robotic and distant; and I knew I had some work to do if I wanted to deepen my experience of life.

When I began to let go of the need for approval from others, my perfectionist tendencies started to melt away. My sense of self-worth grew, eventually making it easier to share the truth of who I was and what I was going through with the world. My self-confidence skyrocketed because I was not relying on what anyone else would think. This ultimately led to the creation of incredible relationships, steeped in deep trust and authenticity, which are at the heart of a joyful life.

Strangely, we all unconsciously look for vulnerability in others, yet we are usually unwilling to be vulnerable ourselves. We see "perfect" individuals as facades of who they really are, and we instinctively feel a sense of distrust, because they provide no messy human stuff for us to relate to. Because we don't feel as if we can trust such individuals, we keep those relationships at arm's length. On the contrary, when people share their messy humanness with us, we connect on a deeper level because we see their vulnerability and trust that they are being open about who they are, rather than trying to hide themselves from us.

When it comes to our own vulnerability, we may initially feel as though we won't be accepted or will be judged for our openness, but usually, it's the opposite that happens. When we're open and vulnerable, people relate to us and feel an instant bond because of our willingness to share, which ultimately gives them the permission to do the same. Both parties can breathe a sigh of relief that they don't have to "have it all together," allowing the real versions of who they are to show up.

I'm reminded of this lesson every time I facilitate The Naked Truth, a workshop that I created with my partner. As part of this workshop, participants reveal their deepest secrets, fears, and insecurities, and we set this portion up so that there is nowhere to hide (physically and emotionally). We created this because we recognized how much energy it takes to hide who we really are. Our physical bodies hold this energy, thereby taking up room in which we could be creating space for magic to happen.

The participants are initially scared to death of this portion of the work, but by the time the session ends and everyone has had a chance to share, they realize something incredible has happened. They see that most people are dealing with similar fears, doubts, secrets, and insecurities, and everyone in the room bonds on a profound level because of this connection. They recognize that when they show up as their TRUE selves, not only do they create a feeling of energetic freedom, but they create deep and meaningful connections and trust with everyone in the room.

True vulnerability and openness is a rare and beautiful thing; that's why it's incredibly special when it's shared. Sure, it's SUPER scary to initially put ourselves out there in a way that we might not be used to, but when we let go of the need for approval, we give ourselves permission to be fully who we are . . . and that feels pretty darn good. We're all human and we all have our messy bits, but that's what makes us who we are. So don't hide yourself; embrace your vulnerability, and don't be afraid to shine.

YOUR MISSION: What is something that you would usually be afraid to admit to someone about yourself?

_____

_____

Who is ONE person you can share this with today?

_____

_____

REFLECTION: How did it feel to show up honestly as the true you? What was the result of your openness?

_____

_____

_____

_____

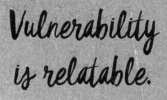

*Vulnerability
is relatable.*

PERFECTION

IS NOT.

#50WaysToYay

29. TURN FAILURE INTO FUEL

Do you know which All-Star basketball player didn't make the varsity team his sophomore year in high school? That would be Michael Jordan. He turned not making the team into his driving fuel . . . his spark. He knew that this moment was going to define him: he could either quit the game altogether or step his game up 1,000 percent and become one of the hardest-working athletes of his generation. And now he's a legend on and off the court.

Similarly, Thomas Edison famously "failed" ten thousand times before he and his team of inventors created a lightbulb that actually worked. He welcomed failure with joy, because the additional knowledge of what wasn't working meant that he was one step closer to finding something that would work.

Unfortunately, our society glorifies the "wins" and rarely mentions the hard work, setbacks, and seeming failures that these men and women of greatness had to endure to get to where they are. This lends to a culture that believes in overnight success and avoiding failure at all costs. We're so afraid of failing that we quit when we are just getting started, or sometimes never even start at all. (See Lesson 9, Be a Person of Persistence.)

But knowing that these legends failed again and again, and eventually rose to success by turning their failures into fuel, means that *we can, too*. We can learn to reframe our failures as experiments and keep persisting until we hit our own "Air Jordan" moment in life.

HOW TO TURN YOUR FAILURE INTO FUEL

1. Expect it and then reframe it.

Failures are a part of life. They are an essential element to moving forward and going after what you want. If you're not failing, you're not acting or being bold enough to try anything new! So expect failures. Welcome them in. It means you're growing, stretching, and trying new things. When we can reframe failure as experimentation on the path to success, this instantly takes the sting of fear away.

2. How are you responsible for it?

Take a giant step back from the situation and honestly ask yourself what role you played in this failed experiment. Were you not present enough? Did you not show up fully or give it your all? Were you playing victim and waiting for others to do the work rather than taking initiative? Bottom line is, we're all at fault SOMEHOW, and in order to move forward more powerfully to the next experiment, we must be willing to call ourselves out about the last one.

3. Find the lesson.

Every failure is a lesson waiting to be discovered. If something went wrong, ask yourself what you learned from it. Find the breakthrough in the breakdown, and take away a golden nugget that will only make you better in the long run.

4. Add fuel to the flame.

Let that setback be your driving force to move closer to what *will* work in your life. Take a different route or put more of yourself into it. Recommit to being your best, showing up fully and playing with all you've got.

5. Release and receive.

In order to create room for the things we want in life, we must be willing to release what hasn't been working (our failures) so we have room to invite in what *will* work. So don't stay stuck on what didn't work, move on and make way for what will.

6. Get honest feedback, and then apply it.

Have someone on your side that you can count on for honest feedback. Find out what you could've done better, what needs a little sharpening, and what areas you might have missed. We all have blind spots, and we need someone else to shine a light on them. Once you know what to focus on, apply, apply, apply!

7. Better your best.

Never get too comfortable with your last success; that is the ULTIMATE failure. Always push for a new record, a new benchmark, a new "top." Going outside your comfort zone and continuing to challenge yourself are keys to fueling the flame. This gives you something to work toward, which will continue to ignite your passion and drive.

So next time you find that you're beating yourself up for not being perfect due to a failure, know that you're at a signpost on the road to success. Reframe your thoughts on failure and watch how it starts to shift your results. Let's turn our failures into fuel and allow them to teach us so that we can move forward better, stronger, and faster. Failure isn't game over—it's GAME ON.

YOUR MISSION: Today, notice when feelings of failure come up. Go through the seven-step process above and turn that failure into fuel.

1. Expect it and then reframe it.
2. How are you responsible for it?
3. Find the lesson.
4. Add fuel to the flame.
5. Release and receive.
6. Get honest feedback, and then apply it.
7. Better your best.

REFLECTION: How did it feel to turn your failure into fuel? What new insights or discoveries were created?

_____

_____

_____

_____

_____

_____

_____

_____

Turn
your failure
into
FUEL.

#50WaysToYay

WHAT ARE YOU

pretending

<u>NOT</u> TO KNOW?

#50WaysToYay

30. WHAT ARE YOU PRETENDING NOT TO KNOW?

Ever have that nagging feeling inside, begging you to do something differently? Ever look back on decisions you've made in the past and say, "I should've trusted my gut"? We've all been there at least once (or if you're like me, you've been there a thousand times), when we intrinsically know what we *should* do, but we ignore all the signals because we don't want to stir things up. We ignore the feeling that something just isn't right, and we resist change out of fear of making the wrong decision. We stay in a relationship way past its expiration date, we don't speak up when we feel something is off, and we ignore obvious signs telling us it's time to change something. Often we feel that if we did what we knew we ought to be doing, it would force us out of our comfort zone; and our comfort zone feels too darn cozy to leave. Listening to our inner knowledge would mean diving headfirst into the unknown; and while that may sound scary, it's often exactly what we need to do in order to be happy.

When we avoid getting real about what's NOT working in our lives, it's as if we are removing the batteries from the fire alarm just as it's going off. There's a fire somewhere that needs to be put out, but we don't like the noise of the alarm, so we take out the batteries and pretend that everything's okay instead. Meanwhile, the fire continues to rage until we actually FACE it and handle it. Our lives are constantly producing symptoms (smoke) that point to a deep-rooted issue (a fire) that needs to be addressed. Our feelings of depression could result from our being disconnected from our purpose; the short fuse we exhibit could stem from an issue we're not willing to address or forgive.

So whenever you feel stuck or stagnant in a situation, or are experiencing symptoms that don't feel so great, ask yourself, "What am I pretending not to know?" Then have the courage to actually listen to the answer and be brave enough to take action.

YOUR MISSION: What is one area of your life in which you feel torn or stuck or are experiencing a negative symptom?

_____

_____

What are you pretending not to know in this situation?

_____

_____

_____

_____

REFLECTION: What are you going to do now that you know what you ought to be doing?

_____

_____

_____

_____

_____

_____

_____

_____

31. SAY NO TO YES

In our busy world, we are now more accessible than ever. People can reach us on email, by text, by instant messenger, on a barrage of social media platforms, on the phone, and yes, they can still get to us in person. That's why it's absolutely critical to hold our time as sacred and get really great at saying no if we want to maintain our levels of peace, presence, and happiness.

When we say yes to others, we're often saying no to ourselves. Saying yes to everyone and everything out of a feeling of obligation or a fear of missing out takes away from how we *actually* want to spend our time. The truth is, when we know what really matters to us, it's a lot easier to say no to all the things that aren't in alignment with our values.

Learning to say no has been critical for my happiness—and my sanity. For the longest time, my people-pleasing tendencies had me worried about keeping my friends and loved ones happy, meanwhile sacrificing my own happiness and self-care in the process. I would constantly be there for others to support them through tough times, to help them build their business, or simply to hang out, leaving no time for what I said I wanted to create in life. Don't get me wrong, I LOVE giving my time and support to the people I care about, but I had to take a long, hard look in the mirror and realize that my care of others shouldn't stand in the way of my care of self.

At first this process was extremely painful. I hated saying no because I feared my friends would make that mean something about our relationship. But as my commitment to building out my vision grew, I soon discovered that my no didn't have anything to do with THEM, and it had everything to do with my vision. Now I can easily tell my friends no because I'm saying yes to something else: I'm committed to creating and sharing what's in my heart, and that's my focus right now. This allows the people in my life to get a deeper understanding of my current focus and my values, and takes away any feelings of guilt over turning down opportunities.

So take stock of what's really important to you, and start saying no to the things that will take you further away from what really matters in your life. Say no without guilt, knowing that you are saying yes to a commitment you've made to yourself. Remember, it's what we say no to, not what we say yes to, that shows what we're *really* committed to.

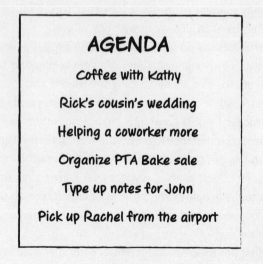

AGENDA

Coffee with Kathy

Rick's cousin's wedding

Helping a coworker more

Organize PTA Bake sale

Type up notes for John

Pick up Rachel from the airport

YOUR MISSION: What are three things in your life that you value most at this time? (Examples: your family, your health, your finances, pursuing your passion in life, nurturing relationships with friends, finding or deepening a committed relationship, etc.)

1. _____

2. _____

3. _____

For the next week, say no to whatever doesn't bring you closer to what you wrote above. The next seven days are all about creating a schedule and a lifestyle that embrace these values, which in turn will empower and excite you to move closer to them.

REFLECTION: How did it feel to say no to others and say yes to yourself?

Say
NO to others
so you can
say YES
to yourself.

#50WaysToYay

Become
A MASTER
of your mornings.

#50WaysToYay

32. MASTER YOUR MORNINGS

What do you do when you first wake up? Check your email? Scroll through social media and check out what your friends are up to? Or do you hit the snooze button and postpone waking up altogether?

Chances are you're not using your morning to its fullest potential. A good friend of mine, Hal Elrod, wrote an amazing book called *The Miracle Morning* that speaks to this exact topic. In his book, Hal shares his incredible wisdom about what got him out of a funk after barely surviving a head-on crash with a drunk driver, being literally dead for six minutes and in a coma for almost a week. It was all about the power of creating meaningful habits and using the quiet, sacred morning time to make sure it happens.

Why the mornings? Well, once you leave your bedroom, the world (your emails, your family, your job, your lists, your dog) all seem to want a bit of your time. But if you claim it, the morning can be all yours. Hal suggests you make your Miracle Morning happen before eight a.m.; some of my closest friends make sure to get their morning ritual in before the sun even rises.

This is something I've practiced on and off for years—but when I actually DO my morning ritual, I am unstoppable. And as my life gets busier, I rely more than ever on my morning ritual to start my day off powerfully. Trying to inspire and empower people into their greatness—starting with myself—is no small feat . . . and I need all the support I can get. So if you want to know my little secret for kicking butt in life, it's the following morning ritual.

MY MORNING RITUAL

0–10 minutes: CONNECTING: Snuggling with my partner.

10–20 minutes: MEDITATION.

20–30 minutes: AFFIRMATIONS + VISUALIZATION.

30–40 minutes: WRITING. Brain Dump (clearing whatever is on my mind) and Gratitude.

40–50 minutes: LEARN. Read for ten minutes or watch an informative or inspiring video online that gives me something to focus on for the day.

50–60 minutes: GET CLEAR ABOUT WHAT I AM CREATING. Writing down in my calendar my Daily Intention (the overarching way I want to create my day), one Daily Stretch (one action that feels uncomfortable but I KNOW will expand what I'm creating in the world), and the TOP THREE things to accomplish today (starting with the scariest one!) that will bring me closer to my vision.

Yes, this may seem overwhelming, but it takes EXTRAORDINARY action to yield EXTRAORDINARY results. It's been documented time and again that the most successful people in the world have routines and rituals that they carve out time for and build their life around. Remember, what initially feels like a struggle and a total inconvenience will eventually be the thing you MUST make happen every day because it leaves you feeling so darn good. It's like brushing your teeth; as a child it was a pain to do, and now you do it because you feel better after doing it—and let's be honest, it's for the general well-being of everyone around you!

So if you think you're really ready to reach new levels of success and joy in your life, it begins with mastering your mornings.

YOUR MISSION: What rituals could you add into your day that would create more joy, presence, and growth in your life? How much time can you commit to each one?

1. _____ **Time:** _____
2. _____ **Time:** _____
3. _____ **Time:** _____

Create time in your day to start at least one of your new rituals.

REFLECTION: How did it feel to carve out time specifically for YOU today?

_____

_____

_____

_____

33. YOUR PRESENCE IS REQUESTED

In life, the most powerful gift we can give anyone at any given moment is our complete presence. In fact, the biggest gripe most people have about their relationships or place of employment is that they feel they aren't being listened to or respected. As human beings, deep down we all want to be seen, heard, and loved; we want to feel respected and valued. And when we show up fully present to those around us, it indicates that we really care and value those we're with.

For years I was a horrendous listener. I was never fully present with the people around me because I was too caught up in my own thoughts, judgments, and opinions. Someone would be sharing his thoughts on a particular subject with me and I would be formulating an answer or rebuttal in my mind, all while putting on my best "listening" face/shaking my head in agreement, and squinting my eyes ever so slightly. I never allowed myself to be fully present to what the other person was saying because I was making sure I had my own two cents cued up and ready to go. Then, in true hypocritical fashion, I would feel disrespected or slighted when someone did the same to me or was on the phone during our time together. How could that other person be so disrespectful?! Funny how we tend to get exactly what we put out, isn't it?

When I finally was able to quiet the chatter in my mind, turn off all distractions, and commit to being present, I felt like I got to know the people around me on a much deeper level. I was able to really hear them and could listen for the subtext under what they were saying, what they were *really* speaking about. Our bonds deepened, and it felt incredible being able to show up and really be there for the people I cared about. Now I practice this level of presence with everyone I meet. I'm not always at my best, but it's something I'm committed to always cultivating because it's such a beautiful gift that we can all give to one another.

So do your best to pay attention—REALLY listen (like, really). Engage and respond spontaneously, without an answer already prepared. Make eye contact with the person you're engaging with and ask meaningful questions to show you're genuinely interested. We're all searching for someone to truly hear us, so be that person for others in your life.

YOUR MISSION: When engaging with people today, truly BE with them. Turn off all distractions and quiet your mind. Hear what's really being said underneath the surface conversation. Look them in the eyes when they're speaking to you and really engage with them. Take a second to respond to what they said, maybe even asking for clarification or posing follow-up questions to show you're truly interested. Keep the conversation focused on them, without adding your opinion or personal anecdotes.

REFLECTION: How did it feel to be truly present with someone today? Was it hard not to revert to old habits and want to add

WHAT
magic
WILL YOU EXPERIENCE

TODAY?

#50WaysToYay

34. WHAT MAGIC WILL YOU EXPERIENCE TODAY?

What we seek, we will eventually find.

Confession: I used to be the Champion of Complaints. I would find myself asking, "Why does this always happen to me? Why can't I find someone I want to be with? Why is it so hard to find people who understand me?" I would constantly try to out-complain every person I saw at work: "Oh, you think THAT'S bad, wait until I tell you about MY sob story!" I was drowning in a sea of negativity and wondered why my happiness indicator was at rock bottom.

Then I learned a key phrase that would change everything for me: WHAT YOU FOCUS ON EXPANDS. Here I was, spending all this time complaining about what wasn't working in my life, not realizing that I was the one actually bringing many of those complaints into my awareness. As woo-woo as this principle sounded to me at first, I gave it a shot and decided to put it to the test.

First, I chose something simple and completely objective: red cars. That day I counted upwards of thirty of them! Now, did there just so happen to be more red cars on the road that day than the day before? Probably not. I simply gave my mind an object to focus on, and it went searching for that object. The next day I decided to go a little crazier and try it with something harder to find in the concrete jungle of New York City: a sea turtle. I went nearly the entire day without seeing ONE sea turtle. Then, on my way home from work, just as I was about ready to throw in the towel on this principle, I saw posters for a kids' movie that had just come out, the main character of which was an animated sea turtle. And then, as if the Universe felt it necessary to knock out any remaining doubt, I received a promotional card in the mail that night about a trip to Mexico. On it was a picture of a couple snorkeling with sea turtles! As you can imagine, I was pretty impressed. (Well played, Universe. Well played.) This was a clear sign that I needed to refocus my energy and attention on the good in my life so I could start attracting more of it.

While red cars and sea turtles are fine and dandy, they're rather specific and limiting. To begin my new practice of positivity, I wanted to find a phrase or question that I could start each and every day off with—a mantra of sorts that would open up a plethora of amazing possibilities for my life. I wanted it to focus on the good, find the amazing, and leave room for unexpected surprises. So the question I began to ask myself was "What magic will I experience today?"

Since putting this into practice, I have seen my world expand exponentially. Starting my day off with that question sends my subconscious mind on a scavenger hunt to FIND THE MAGIC in each and every moment. And good news . . . it's *everywhere*. So if you want to experience more joy, bliss, abundance, and MAGIC in your life, you've got to get bold and *ask for it*. You've got to focus your energy on what IS working so you can bring more of that goodness into your awareness. Once you start looking for it, you'll begin to see it unfold in EVERYTHING.

YOUR MISSION: Before you leave the house, as you enter work, or whenever you find yourself about to ask a disempowering question, instead ask yourself, "What magic will I experience today?"

REFLECTION: What magic occurred for you today? What did this exercise open up for you?

_____

_____

_____

_____

_____

_____

_____

35. ACKNOWLEDGE ABUNDANCE

YOU: I want more money.

THE UNIVERSE: Okay, cool. So why do you keep ignoring all those coins I leave you on the street?

YOU: Oh, come on! That doesn't count. I want REAL money.

THE UNIVERSE (*SHAKING ITS GIGANTIC HEAD*): And you wonder why I don't give you more, you ungrateful fool!

Abundance is *everywhere*. Whether or not we choose to see it is *our* problem. When we start paying attention to all of the abundance that surrounds us, we inevitably get more of it. If we emphasize that we want more money, the mere focus on *wanting* is a declaration that we don't have it yet. So we must practice acknowledging all of the incredible abundance *already* around us. It's in nature, in our food, in information, in our access to people all over the world, in our plethora of choices, and yes, even in money. We are surrounded by abundance because we live in an abundant Universe. When we focus on the abundance that *is* the Universe, we open the floodgates for more of that abundance to pour in.

So as crazy as it sounds, I pick up *every* single coin that I see on the ground, smile, and thank the Universe for its generosity. It's one of my little reminders that abundance is all around me.

YOUR MISSION: Take notice of the abundance all around you today. Be grateful for what the Universe has provided you with. Keep a special eye out for any coins that you find on the ground, and pick them up with a smile and an unspoken thank you.

REFLECTION: What did you notice about the abundance that surrounds you?

_____

_____

_____

_____

_____

_____

_____

_____

Acknowledge
the abundance
THAT SURROUNDS YOU.

#50WaysToYay

One moment

CAN CHANGE

THE ENTIRE COURSE

OF OUR LIVES.

#50WaysToYay

36. ALL IT TAKES IS ONE

We are NEVER stuck where we currently are. Transformation can literally happen in a moment . . . in a spark. All it takes is one conversation, one song, one meditation, one hug, one smile, one book, one walk in nature—ONE CHOICE to do or say something different that could literally change everything.

The beauty of this life is that not only are we able to affect our own reality based on the choices we make, but we also have the incredible ability to completely shift someone else's. Every action we take and every word we speak has an effect—either positive or negative. By shooting someone a smile or offering her encouraging words during a difficult time, we can literally change the course of her entire day, and therefore her life for the better. On the other hand, we have the power to kill someone's dreams in an instant or hurt someone with the power of our words alone.

Knowing that everything we put out in the world has an effect, I became super intentional about *my* words and actions. I decided that I wanted to be a positive catalyst for others, rather than a negative one, and so began a habit that is now a huge part of my business. I love to share quotes or ideas from what I'm currently reading or learning with others; and with the birth of social media, I now get to share those bursts of inspiration with a global audience through videos, blogs, and inspirational pictures that I post online. People from around the world have sent me countless messages saying that just one particular post changed the entire course of their lives—ONE post! That certainly feels a lot more positive than the effect my words and actions *used* to create.

So get super intentional with your words and your actions, knowing that every single one of them will produce an effect in you and in others. Today, do ONE thing differently that will start a domino effect of positive change in your world or offer to be the spark of something amazing for someone else.

YOUR MISSION: Today, make ONE choice in your words or with your actions that could be a catalyst for a new way of living for yourself or someone else; be the spark for something incredible.

REFLECTION:
What new shift did you create for yourself or someone else today?

_____

_____

_____

_____

_____

_____

_____

_____

NO
simply means
NEXT OPPORTUNITY.

#50WaysToYay

37. OPEN MOUTHS GET FED

We must communicate our needs and desires in order for them to be met.

For the longest time, I felt like asking for *anything* was the scariest thing in the world to do. I didn't want to make others feel uncomfortable or come across as too pushy or needy. I felt that by expressing my needs to others I was being a massive pain in the butt, so I would just continue along without asking for support and would eventually end up resenting that I never received the support I secretly wanted. I was so deathly afraid of hearing no that I just avoided the conversation altogether; if I never asked, I would hopefully never have to hear that terrifying word!

This was a negative factor for me in business partnerships and also in my relationships. I would secretly want the other person to behave in a certain way or to offer me support, but I didn't want to have to ask for it. I wrongfully believed that if others truly cared about me, they would *know* what I needed them to do. Although I felt totally entitled to my feelings at the time (shocking, I know!), to expect *anyone* to read my mind is pretty ridiculous. Once I became aware of the utter ridiculousness of my expectations, I was able to make some changes.

I began to share my needs and concerns with others. I began to ask for support when I needed it. I began to communicate my feelings in a way that wasn't laced with judgment or blame. I learned to make clear requests and be okay with a response of yes *or* no. I realized that if I made a request without giving people the freedom to say no, then they never had the freedom to say yes in the first place. I no longer thought that if I was told no, it meant that someone was rejecting me; it simply meant it was time to move on to the next opportunity. This freed me up to reframe my requests or find alternative methods to getting my needs met. In all areas of my life—from scaling my business to having a relationship in which I feel heard and supported—I have found that the art of asking has truly proven to be a game changer.

So if we really want to live life with more *YAY!*, we've got to be willing to speak up. We will never get what we desire if we don't have the courage to ask for it. We have to be willing to trust ourselves enough to make requests and then be open and flexible with the responses we receive. The more we practice the art of asking, the better at it we'll become.

YOUR MISSION: What feelings of resentment have you let build up, waiting for the moment when someone will eventually "get the hint"?

_____

_____

_____

_____

What clear request were you unwilling to make?

_____

_____

_____

_____

Find time today to make a clear request, from an open and flexible place. Be the space for the other person to say yes or no, and remember, if the person turns down your request, this does not mean he is rejecting you; it simply means it's time to move on to the next opportunity.

REFLECTION: How did it feel to take ownership of where you would like more support in your life?

_____

_____

_____

_____

What transpired after you spoke up?

_____

_____

_____

_____

_____

_____

_____

38. HAVE I TOLD YOU LATELY?

A little acknowledgment goes a LONG way. It has the ability to completely transform your relationships in an *instant*, and best of all it's free, it's easy, and it feels spectacular. It's a really simple thing to do, yet often gets overlooked out of the assumption that people "already know" how much you care about and appreciate them. No matter how much you assume that they already know how you feel, remind them. It will make those you care about feel absolutely incredible, and that magical energy of love and gratitude will leave you feeling pretty awesome, too.

I learned an incredibly easy and effective formula for masterful appreciation from one of my mentors, Scott Coady, founder of the Institute of Embodied Wisdom. I really like this method of appreciation because it feels grounded and really lands with others. Because you're giving other people specific statements about how and why you appreciate them and what they mean to you, it's harder for their inner critic to dismiss what you say or brush it off as "smoke-blowing."

1. Acknowledge what they did that you appreciate.
2. Specifically name the qualities they possess to make them someone that you admire.
   a. Speak to the virtues of the person.
   b. Praise what they do that you would like to cultivate more of.

c. Acknowledge specific attributes that contributed to their admirable behavior.

3. Share WHY you appreciate them.

a. Give them context so they don't make up their own.

b. What does it mean to you personally that they are this amazing?

c. What does it mean for the world?

YOUR MISSION: Choose one person that you see or speak to all the time and tell them in person or over the phone how much they mean to you, how incredible they are, and how much you just needed to let them know, for no reason at all. If you're up for it, use the model for appreciation I shared with you above to really ground your acknowledgment.

REFLECTION: How did this make you feel?

_____

_____

_____

_____

Did anything new open up in the relationships you shared your appreciation for?

_____

_____

_____

_____

_____

_____

_____

ACKNOWLEDGMENT
IS *food*
FOR THE *soul.*

#50WaysToYay

39. BLESSED TO

You know all those things you HAVE to do? You know, wake up early to get to work on time, pay the rent, cook dinner, do the laundry, clean the house, study for class, go to the bank, go through the mail, *and* take the dog out? Well, you actually don't HAVE to do any of them. Great news, right?

First, doing *anything* in this world is a CHOICE; we have the option to do it or to not do it. Sure, there are consequences for our actions, but it is still a choice that *we* get to make. Of course, certain things in life—like paying bills and feeding our family—seem pretty important to do, so how can we reframe those things so as to make them more enjoyable and bring more *YAY!* to our days?

When we start with the idea that we don't HAVE to do anything, but instead are BLESSED to do it, we are reminded that not only is it our *choice* to embark on that task, but it's an absolute honor and blessing that we are alive and capable of choosing to do it. Coming from a place of gratitude for our daily to-dos actually moves our mind toward finding the best and most enjoyable route to accomplish it. The phrase "I have to" instantly creates stress and annoyance. By reframing this as "I'm BLESSED to," we create a feeling of joy, empowerment, and gratitude as we navigate this gift of life.

YOUR MISSION: Today, reframe your language from "I HAVE to" to "I'm BLESSED to." It might be hard at first, but just keep catching and adjusting yourself throughout the day.

REFLECTION: How did this subtle shift in language affect your overall mood and energy today?

_____

_____

_____

_____

_____

_____

_____

_____

CHANGE YOUR LANGUAGE.
Change your life.

#50WaysToYay

Instead of asking,
"WHAT DOES THE WORLD
HAVE FOR ME?"

ASK,
"What do I have
for the world?"

#50WaysToYay

40. BE A GO-GIVER

Is your hand up or out? Are you creating value *for* the world, or consuming and taking value *from* it? You have to be willing to GIVE more in order to GET more in life, and those with their hand out rarely experience what true abundance feels like.

Takers are people who try to get as much from others as possible, with the intent *to get* something out of a situation. Givers are those who go out of their way to offer support, while expecting nothing in return. Not only is coming from a taker mentality completely disempowering, but people generally don't like takers. But do you know what people DO love? A giver.

People want to help out the person who's always got their back. This is the basis of the law of reciprocity: when someone supports us, we have a deep-rooted psychological urge to return the favor. In fact, we may even reciprocate the initial favor with one far greater to show just how appreciative we are. Now, the law of reciprocity is NOT the reason we should be inclined to give. Trust me, there is nothing more unattractive than someone who is a taker at heart pretending to be a generous giver. However, if we can find a way to genuinely SERVE, we create a flow of GIVING energy in our lives.

I have always truly enjoyed giving. I love supporting others whenever possible, as it sincerely lights me up to see people flourish. I believe that it's my duty to share whatever it is that I have learned that may be of value to others, and to help lift others up and create value in the world whenever I can. Because this has always been a part of who I am, the law of reciprocity has been kind to me. People seem to be willing to go above and beyond when I need them, and I feel as if opportunities are practically banging down my door.

When we hoard our time, talents, support, or love, we send out a message of scarcity to the world that there's not enough to go around. Like a magnet, this message finds more "not enough" and brings it our way. But if we give freely of our resources, it creates a vibration of generosity and abundance, which in turn creates and attracts an endless cycle of flow into our lives. So be in the practice of entering into each situation, relationship, or business deal as a Go-GIVER: with your hand up, asking, "How can I support you or serve in this situation?" This one simple move makes you the most popular kid on the block, and it feels pretty darn good, too.

YOUR MISSION: Challenge yourself to ask three different people, "How can I support you?" It may feel weird at first, but you'll get into a flow and these words will become like second nature to you.

REFLECTION: How did people react to your offering of support?

_____

_____

_____

_____

How did it make you feel to be there for others?

_____

_____

_____

_____

_____

_____

_____

_____

41. LET'S TALK ABOUT YOUR FEELINGS, SHALL WE?

Goals are not all they're cracked up to be. Yup, I said it. This, coming from the woman who was a goal-setting machine. I read almost every book about achieving success through concrete goals, and when I was in my early twenties, my mom and I even cowrote a book that touched on the importance of setting goals.

But alas, my views have changed. Yes, studies of goal-setting reveal that goals are effective in helping us achieve what we set out to achieve, but these same studies don't really talk about what happens when we get to the top of the mountain. It's called the Depression of Success, the "IS THIS ALL THERE IS?" Syndrome. We are so dead set on getting to the top of our chosen mountain that we put all our faith in THAT mountaintop being the answer to making our life better. Then we reach the summit, and a lackluster feeling starts to set in after the initial glory fades. So how do we beat this?

Well, MOST people set goals based on what their ego wants, and not necessarily for what their lives were divinely constructed for. If we're holding too firmly to a particular goal we've set out to achieve—to be a famous entertainer, to be an incredible business leader, to earn X dollars in Y years, to be married with kids by thirty-three—we have no room in our "energetic hands" to take hold of what might be right in front of us—what might perhaps be better suited for living out our highest potential.

I can totally relate to this, because at one time I was SO fixated on achieving my goals in television and modeling that I wasn't paying attention to whether these goals FELT right for me. I just HAD to get to the finish line of the race I had started, *no matter what*. Now that I've let go of the notion of "making it" in any field, my TRUE path has unfolded before me, and (quite frankly) was there the whole time waiting for me to notice it. I could've never guessed or worked toward the goal of becoming what I do now, because the vision that I am living out currently didn't even exist five years ago!

I'm not saying goals are BAD—they're great. Nine times out of ten, if we're diligent, the parameters of our goal will help guide us directly to the finish line; it just may not be as fulfilling as we thought it would be when we get there. Why is that? Well, in my experience working with thousands of people around the world, I've come to notice that the goal they set for themselves wasn't necessarily what they truly wanted in the first place. What we're *really* after is the FEELING the accomplishment of that goal will bring.

So it's not about the award-winning career, it's about feeling worthy and respected in society. It's not about attracting our soul mate, but about feeling connection and love. It's not about having a million bucks in the bank, a luxury car, and a mansion in the most desirable neighborhood; it's about feeling that we're valuable. Once we get that we're actually after the FEELING and not the goal itself, we can start experiencing those feelings with or without the goals actually being met.

Most people assume that if we HAVE what we want, we'll

be able to DO more and ultimately BE more. If we have the money, we'll be able to travel and feel more free and happy in life. But this is not necessarily true. We all know people who supposedly have it all who aren't happy, aren't fulfilled, don't feel worthy, and don't feel a sense of love in their lives. So we've got to flip the formula: instead of HAVE, DO, BE, it's BE, DO, HAVE.

We must *first* BE what we want (happy, worthy, enough, love, significant) and then DO or act from that space of being, which in turn will attract what we want to HAVE in life. It's about showing up as how we want to FEEL, then taking actions based on that place of being, so that we begin attracting scenarios that validate our state of being. Whether you ever reach those goals or not, you'll still be happy, fulfilled, and joyous regardless . . . if you choose to BE IT first.

So no matter what goals you may have set for yourself, I urge you to look a little deeper and ask what FEELING you're actually after. Then BE what you want to feel RIGHT NOW and you'll see that success has always been just a choice away.

YOUR MISSION: List three of the goals you have for your life and the feelings that you are really after underneath these goals.

Example:

GOAL: I want to make six figures this year.

FEELINGS: Security, freedom, and respect.

GOAL: _____

FEELINGS: _____

GOAL: _____

FEELINGS: _____

GOAL: _____

FEELINGS: _____

REFLECTION: Now that you're clear on the FEELINGS you're truly after, how can you CHOOSE TO BE those feelings NOW?

_____

_____

_____

_____

_____

_____

_____

_____

YOU CANNOT ATTRACT

WHAT YOU ARE NOT
willing to BE.

#50WaysToYay

CHANGE

YOUR

baseline
for goodness.

#50WaysToYay

42. TURN UP THE BASE

If you won the lottery tomorrow, would you instantly be happier? You probably said yes, but researchers would disagree.

Studies have found that no matter what levels of happiness and success we're experiencing in life, we tend to return to a fixed baseline, a set point that we are comfortable with being at. This baseline remains the same unless a person makes a strong effort to change it.

A great example of this is people who win the lottery. They often start off with a baseline of success and happiness that's far below that of their lottery-winning new state, generally going from humble five-figure salaries to millions of dollars overnight. While the winners' levels of happiness spiked after they initially won the money, these levels usually returned to their pre-winning state after just a few months. In fact, upwards of 70 percent of lottery winners eventually end up broke and financially back to where they started before their winnings, because that's what they're used to.

Gay Hendricks describes a great metaphor for this in his amazing book *The Big Leap:* "Each of us has an inner thermostat setting that determines how much love, success, and creativity we allow ourselves to enjoy. When we exceed our inner thermostat setting, we will often do something to sabotage ourselves, causing us to drop back into the old, familiar zone where we feel secure. Unfortunately, our thermostat setting usually gets programmed in early childhood, before we can think for ourselves."

Whew! When I read that, boy, did it hit home. I instantly thought of all the times a massive opportunity would come my way and I would somehow, some way find a ridiculous way to sabotage it. Even more, I flashed back to all those times I picked a fight for no good reason at all with my partner when things were going great, and realized that it was likely because my inner thermostat was pushing a little too far past my set point. The good news is, we have control of our inner thermostat and with a little effort, patience, and commitment we can turn up our baseline "temperature." By becoming aware of our internal saboteurs, we can stop them dead in their tracks. Although I've become quite friendly with my saboteurs (worrying what others will think and making mountains out of molehills), I consciously have to keep manually overriding my gauge's default settings and raising the temperature over and over again.

With practices like feeling gratitude (Lesson 20), becoming friends with fear (Lesson 4), and focusing on your vision (Lesson 14), you'll be well on your way to knocking out your saboteurs, turning up your baseline of goodness, and setting a new standard for joy in your life.

YOUR MISSION: Today, notice any saboteurs that seem to pop up right as you accomplish a big win, experience an overflow of joy, or realize that you haven't fought with your loved one in a while.

REFLECTION: Did you notice any moments where your inner thermostat tried to kick in and bring you back to your baseline? What did you notice about your saboteurs?

_____

_____

_____

_____

_____

_____

_____

_____

BE STILL, AND *listen.*

#50WaysToYay

43. THE POWER OF SILENCE

In case you haven't heard by now, meditation is pretty powerful. For thousands of years, people have been using meditation to access more empathy, practice presence, reduce stress, ramp up brainpower, and foster a stronger connection to source energy. Now modern science is finally catching on.

Research has shown that a regular practice of meditation reduces anxiety and depression, strengthens the immune system, improves memory, heightens our self-awareness, and increases empathy. It reduces negative feelings of sadness, tension, and anger. Meditation encourages conscious use of the mind's faculties. So why isn't this mandatory for everyone to do? Unfortunately, while a lot of us know meditation is good for us, we still fail to actually *do* it. In the same vein, there are many secrets to success and happiness out there, but very few people are actually WILLING to apply them to their lives. While meditation certainly isn't the only way, it's one of the fastest ones to a deep sense of inner peace and happiness.

Meditation doesn't have to be about sitting in a perfect lotus pose while burning incense next to our crystal shrine. It's not about what we look like while we do it or where our mind "goes to" after we begin. The benefits of meditation are received by simply quieting the mind and becoming aware of our focus. In meditation we observe that thoughts, feelings, and emotions come and go, and are always changing. We realize that we are not our thoughts, feelings, and emotions, but rather the unchanging observer of them; this observer or witness is the Authentic Self. Anchored in the unchanging nature of its essence, this Authentic Self has no titles or labels, has no pressing needs or concerns; it is pure consciousness. If we can commit to as little as one or two minutes a day, we will begin to see results in our way of being with the world and everything in it. And chances are those few minutes will feel so good that adding on a few more eventually won't seem so challenging.

So how badly do you ACTUALLY want to experience more joy, peace, awareness, and harmony in life? If you're reading this book, my guess is that you do want to create more of that in your life. So, it's time to create a little time and make meditation a priority. Meditation is a fast track to experience an inner transformation that will change our way of being in the world and inevitably affect every single aspect of our lives.

YOUR MISSION: Today, set aside a minimum of two minutes to sit in silence with no distractions. Focus on your breath as it enters and leaves the body. Notice whatever thoughts arise without judgment and then refocus back on your breath.

REFLECTION: Knowing that meditation is a game changer, are you willing to carve out time on a daily basis to make this a part of your routine? Why or why not?

_____

_____

_____

_____

44. I WILL DESTROY YOU!

The first act of creation is ALWAYS destruction. A new relationship can blossom only after an old one is complete. The seed must die in order for the tree to grow. A new business venture can start because you've opened up space for it by dedicating time in your evenings or quitting your job. A new character trait can develop and take shape because you've created an opening for it by eliminating an old one that didn't serve you. This lesson is also great to remember right after any major loss that you may face in life, such as a breakup or being let go from your job. Sometimes what you think of as a loss is exactly what is needed to bring in something more aligned for your life.

A really powerful example of this lesson from my own life was when I put in my two-week notice to the bartending job I had. Now this wasn't just any old bartending job—I was working two nights a week in one of the top nightclubs in New York City and making a fortune. To be blunt, it was one of the cushiest gigs I ever had, and it was really hard to walk away from the kind of money I was making. But truth be told, I hated the job. I couldn't stand the late nights, the environment of drinking and drugs, and the smoke and mirrors that went into making it one of the most "exclusive" spots in the city. I worked there as I was building out my career and establishing myself in television, and I knew deep down that I wasn't going to flourish in TV until I was willing to get rid of this cushy side job that kept me comfortable. Yes, it was great money. Yes, it required very little of my time and energy. And yes, knowing that I always had this job as an option made me work *just* a little less harder than what was needed to really become successful in TV. When I really got honest with myself about this, I put in my notice. I was scared out of my mind to walk away from that kind of money, but I knew it had to happen. Twelve hours after I submitted my letter of resignation, I received a call from a producer friend of mine. He had submitted my name to be considered for a hosting position on a new home-makeover show on HGTV. Now, I had no formal education in home interiors, but I was a complete design hobbyist. Long story short, I was flown to Tennessee with eight other designers to screen-test for this show, and I ended up being booked as the main host. While that show had a great run, it also opened the door to many other amazing television opportunities for me. It was as if the Universe was waiting for me to get rid of my cushy, easy bartending job and be 100 percent committed to making a career in TV happen before it was going to bring this big of an opportunity my way.

Bottom line, we must be willing to give up in order to go up. So what do you want to CREATE in life? What are you willing to give up in order to make that happen? What can you DESTROY that is no longer serving you in order to create space for something new and amazing to emerge? If we want success, we have to be willing to sacrifice. So what are you waiting for: seek, destroy, and create!

YOUR MISSION: What are you looking to create in your life that you don't have yet?

What must you be willing to destroy/stop doing/give up/sacrifice in order to make space for this new creation?

_____

_____

_____

_____

REFLECTION: Remember and reflect on a time in your life when you experienced a major loss (such as a breakup or being let go at work) that turned out to be the beginning of something really incredible.

_____

_____

_____

_____

_____

_____

_____

_____

The first act of creation
is always
DESTRUCTION.

#50WaysToYay

45. YOU'RE SUCH A PEACH

You could be the sweetest, juiciest, most succulent peach the Universe has EVER seen in the history of humankind . . . and someone just might not like peaches.

As a peach, you're going to encounter a bunch of raving peach fans in your lifetime, and boy, will they LOVE you; but not everyone is a fan of peaches.

It's important to know who you are, what you're worth (you're priceless, by the way), and what you stand for. If you are confident about your character and integrity, no one can shake that. If you're sure of your brilliance, nothing will break that down. People will always have their opinions, good and bad, but those opinions will hold no sway over you if you can stand confidently in the magic of your truth. No one can stand in the way of authenticity.

So don't try to become an apple for that apple-loving peach hater. You couldn't even if you tried—you're a peach, after all. So be the most amazing peach the planet has ever seen. Rock that sweetness to the cosmos and back, and let the apple lovers worry about the apples.

YOUR MISSION: In what ways have you tried to become someone or something that you're not in order to please others or fit in?

_____

_____

Do those changes feel authentic to who you truly are? Do you still want to hold on to them? Or are you ready to let them go, knowing they aren't a true representation of you?

_____

_____

_____

_____

REFLECTION: How do you plan to bring more of the authentic YOU into the future?

_____

_____

_____

_____

_____

_____

_____

_____

YOU'LL NEVER BE

everyone's FAVORITE.

#50WaysToYay

46. YOU ARE THE SEED

The strength and majesty of the mighty oak tree is all held within a tiny acorn. And given the proper conditions, that seed will grow into its highest potential. You are that seed; you were specifically designed with everything you need to actualize your full potential. You possess all the strength, joy, intuition, happiness, love, and abundance necessary to achieve what you were destined to do. With the proper care, conditions, and nurturing, your life will eventually grow into its highest potential.

This lesson was expanded on even further for me during a trip I took to Joshua Tree National Park with a group of friends. As I came out of an intense hour-long meditation out in the wilderness, I noticed this beautiful and majestic tree, so full of life, right in the middle of this incredible scenery I was in. I spotted a friend of mine relaxing under the shade of this tree, watched two birds nesting in its foliage, and noticed all the little flowers on the tree that kept the bees busy and happy. All this life, all this purpose, all this contribution . . . from a single seed. The desert needed this tree; it was vital to the entire ecosystem of this area.

We, too, are but a seed. A seed that, once fertilized, took shape and form, and fought its way into BEINGness, just as this tree fought against the elements to fulfill its purpose in the world. We are a seed that has within it everything that's necessary for our growth, our purpose, and our contribution to this life. The problem is, we've forgotten that we are birthed from a seed; and that within this seed, we had not only all that we needed to form and grow the conscious human being reading this, but also all of the potential necessary to bring our BEING-ness through to its full expression. We have it all here within us, but we keep looking outside ourselves, thinking the answer lies somewhere out there. We keep looking to the new career, the new love, the new family, the new house, the new car, the new clothes, the new city, the new experience, the new degree, and the new accomplishments as if those are the things that will pull us into our full potential.

Everything is already written. We, like the tree, have everything we need to reach our full expression. All we have to do is TRUST our makeup, unlock our inner potential, get out of our own way and THRIVE despite the conditions. Most importantly, we must ensure that we have cultivated the proper environment necessary for our highest growth. So choose to surround yourself with amazing people, fill your brain with positivity, fill your soul with messages of love and encouragement, and fuel your body with real food and movement.

Your life is a direct reflection of the ingredients you choose to put into it, and it's our purpose to grow into the highest expression of our Authentic Selves so that we may contribute whatever our gift is to the world.

YOUR MISSION: In what ways can you feed and nourish your:

Mind: _____

Body: _____

Spirit: _____

Health: _____

Relationships: _____

Finances: _____

Passion: _____

What area will you focus on first? Why?

_____

_____

REFLECTION: How does it feel to know that you have everything you need within you to bring you to your fullest potential? What have you let get in the way of your highest growth?

_____

_____

_____

_____

_____

_____

_____

_____

You were born with it all,
but it's up to you
TO CREATE
the right conditions for
growth.

#50WaysToYay

WHAT WOULD

LOVE

DO NOW?

50WaysToYay

47. BE A DISCIPLE OF LOVE

"Disciple" is the root of the word "discipline." It means to learn and grow under the command or teaching of someone or something *at all costs*. So be a DISCIPLE OF LOVE. Learn and grow under LOVE's command at all costs.

In one of my all-time favorite books, *Conversations with God*, author Neale Donald Walsch encapsulates this idea of being under love's command with a simple question: "What would love do now?" This question has served as a reminder for me, time and time again, to be a Disciple of Love even when faced with the toughest of situations. I've used it during difficult conversations. I've used it when passing a homeless man on the street. I've even used it when deciding which direction to go next with my business.

When life's moments get difficult to navigate, a Disciple of Love would grow under Love's command at all costs and ask, "What would love do now?" The ego will consistently put up a good fight, but LOVE wins every time when we choose to allow it.

YOUR MISSION: In what areas of your life is it easy for you to show up as love?

_____

_____

Why?

_____

_____

What areas of your life consistently challenge your ability to show up as love?

_____

_____

Why?

_____

_____

Think of a difficult challenge you're facing. Ask yourself, "What would love do now?" and answer below.

_____

_____

_____

_____

_____

_____

_____

_____

Keep this question of "What would love do now?" in your thoughts as you navigate your day. Notice any opportunities you have to put this question into play and become a Disciple of Love.

REFLECTION: Why is being a Disciple of Love important for your happiness, success, and joy in life? What did you notice when you used the question "What would love do now" today?

_____

_____

_____

_____

_____

_____

_____

_____

48. OWN YOUR BS

Many of us live with limiting belief systems (BS) that say that we just can't have the life we want because of the life we've been given. Well, I beg to differ.

Throughout my years of nonprofit work in some of the poorest areas of the world, I've seen people who were born into absolute poverty pave a path to success for themselves and their families. These amazing people were able to create something out of nothing because they believed themselves to be limitless beings. They resisted the temptation of "I can't," "it could never work," and "woe is me," and with the continued belief of "I will" they persisted until the impossible became possible.

History is filled with people who believed the impossible was possible and made it happen because they *believed* that they could. It's why we are able to enjoy breakthroughs such as the Internet, smartphones, airplanes, and medical miracles. However, most people fail before they even begin because they don't believe, deep down, that their dreams are ACTUALLY possible. On the other hand, some of the most successful people in life aren't necessarily the most skilled or talented in their field; they simply have the strongest belief in themselves and are able to successfully carry out their vision.

Young kids are a beautiful example of this. I have a nephew who is a toddler, and now that he's walking, I can see his subconscious beliefs play out in life. One minute he believes he's a superhero and is shooting spiderwebs out from his hands and doing crazy jumps and tricks. The next minute he's a tank engine and is picking me up to go on an adventure to a magical land. We were all toddlers at some point, and we all were born with the belief that we could do and be anything. As we grew up, we became conditioned by society to "get real," and we started creating limitations on what we believed to be achievable.

Our beliefs are the invisible force controlling all of our decisions and determining how we feel, think, and act throughout our lives. When we believe something, either consciously or unconsciously, we give our brain a command to respond accordingly. That belief takes over and begins to drive what we can see and what we can feel. Some of these beliefs we carry are powerful and truly serve us in life; others are a bit more destructive.

Examples of empowering beliefs are:
- "I can do anything I put my mind to."
- "It's not failure, it's an opportunity to learn."
- "I am a successful person."
- "Love heals everything."

Examples of disempowering beliefs are:
- "I'm no good at this."
- "Money is the root of all evil."
- "I'm a victim of my circumstances."
- "I'll never get ahead."

At any given moment we can choose what we believe about ourselves, and these beliefs will determine the actions we take and the feelings we feel. The more we remind ourselves about our beliefs by reaffirming them, the more they become a part of our identity. This is why it's critical that we become aware of our underlying belief system, own it, and choose to focus on empowering thoughts.

I AM WHAT I SAY I AM

"I AM" are two of the most powerful words we can say. Why? Because what we put after them will shape our reality and manifest what we declare. "I AM" precedes the subconscious beliefs that we program ourselves with, literally telling us how to feel in our body and mind. These words also radiate a frequency to attract an outer reality that matches whatever we choose to insert after the words "I AM." For example, "I am not smart enough" will have us focused on how smart everyone else is, and leave us feeling like we have nothing worthy to contribute. Our belief of "I am shy" will leave us constantly sitting in the stands of life, passively watching as other people play. Every time we use the words "I AM" we are sending instructions to our body and mind to think, feel, and act a certain way. We are directing our subconscious mind to focus on whatever we tell it to focus on, and it literally filters out everything else.

So what are you saying to yourself? Pay close attention to not just your words but also your thoughts. Notice when you use phrases like "I am not good enough," "I am a jealous person," "I am angry," or "I am so tired of it." Notice how we unconsciously create our experience based on these disempowering beliefs. We have the power to create our experience of life based on the words we use, so choose your words wisely.

As you move through life, stand firmly in your declarations of who you are by consciously choosing to put an empowering finish to the statement that begins with "I AM." Some fun ones to try on are powerful, beautiful, wise, creative, capable, strong, insightful, loving, kind, peaceful, compassionate, funny, outgoing, sexy, brilliant. Yup . . . those sound pretty good to me, too.

YOUR MISSION:

What negative belief systems (BS) have been running your life?

1. _____
2. _____
3. _____

How can you reframe those negative beliefs into empowering ones?

1. _____
2. _____
3. _____

Today I declare to myself and to the world that

I AM _____

_____

I AM _____

_____

I AM _____

_____

REFLECTION: How did it feel to powerfully create who you are today with your "I AM" statements and reframed, empowering beliefs?

_____

_____

_____

_____

I am what I say I AM.

#50WaysToYay

49. THE EXTRA MILE

Excellence is the hallmark of all extraordinary people.

Because it's such a rare quality, excellence is what makes people stand out from the crowd. It creates a level of self-trust and self-confidence, which inevitably creates more trust with others. That trust makes us indispensable in our relationships and our work; and it creates a unique stance for whatever vision we're committed to carrying out in the world. We earn a reputation of impeccability, and that's something we can take everywhere with us. When we go the extra mile, others take notice and we set ourselves apart from the rest.

A part of embodying excellence is being a person of integrity. Integrity means doing the right thing at all times, even when no one is watching. It's about honoring the commitments that we've made, showing up as who we say we are, and taking responsibility for our actions. It's about being impeccable in our choice of words, and not using our words to judge or criticize ourselves or others. It's about being intentional in our thoughts, words, and actions and aligning those thoughts, words, and actions with who we say we are and what we're committed to.

While cutting corners may provide a momentary burst of instant gratification, that feeling won't last. Eventually, by doing just enough to get by or by being flat-out dishonest, we erode our self-esteem and ability to trust anyone because we realize we can't even trust ourselves. We begin to identify as a person who doesn't follow through, who lies and cheats, and who lets others down. With that lack of faith in ourselves, we realize that other people ultimately won't trust us, so why follow through in the first place? This sets in motion a negative cycle of disempowering behavior that becomes a self-fulfilling prophecy. We feel untrustworthy, competitive, and downright miserable.

This was something I had to learn about the hard way. As a kid, I noticed that if I lied ever so slightly about certain things, I could keep almost everyone happy. Mom would trust that I completed my chores, and Dad would believe that my homework was finished. My teachers would give me extra time for a project because I lied and said something came up, and my friends' feelings wouldn't get hurt if I didn't want to play with them. My little white lies eventually became habitual, an integral part of who I was. I told so many white lies so often that I couldn't tell what was even true anymore . . . until I got caught. As soon as I got called on one lie, it was as if my entire pre-teen life of lies began to unravel. I felt completely out of control and left a mess of burned relationships in my wake. I realized that if I could never trust myself to be fully honest, how could I ever trust someone else to be? Picking up the pieces was humiliating and awful, and because I never wanted to experience that level of pain again, I decided to commit to being a person of integrity. I would tell the truth, honor my commitments, and hold myself to the highest standards of integrity, no matter what. This wasn't an easy choice, but it has continued to contribute an incredible amount of trust, happiness, and peace to my life.

True happiness, success, and joy come from an inner knowing that we are people of integrity and therefore of excellence. When we are able to stand by our commitments, keep our word, and be truly at peace with who we are, we create an unshakable foundation that can't be touched.

So how are you doing with your commitments? Do you actually follow through on what you say you will? Or do you agree to things simply to be agreeable and then flake later on? How careful are you with your words? Do you use them to create and foster more love, or do you use them to generate more fear, negativity, and hate? Are you acting according to how you say you act, even when no one is watching? We're all human, and no one is perfect; however, when we become aware of our shortcomings, we can begin to take action and choose something different.

If we want more success, happiness, fulfillment, and joy in our lives, we have to be willing to commit to a life of excellence. When we give more than what's expected, we'll always get more than we could have imagined as a result.

YOUR MISSION:

Where in your life are you making a commitment to excellence and integrity?

_____

_____

_____

_____

_____

Where in your life are you NOT making a commitment to excellence and integrity?

_____

_____

_____

_____

How can you give more to what you're already doing and become a person of excellence?

_____

_____

_____

_____

How can you bring integrity and truth to a situation in which you were dishonest or didn't keep your word?

_____

_____

_____

_____

REFLECTION: How does it feel to take an honest look at how you're showing up in life? Are you proud of the person you are behind closed doors? Or did you cringe at the thought of being found out?

_____

_____

_____

_____

_____

_____

_____

BE A PERSON OF
excellence.

#50WaysToYay

THE LIFE YOU LIVE

today

IS THE

legacy

YOU LEAVE BEHIND.

#50WaysToYay

50. WHAT WILL YOU LEAVE BEHIND?

We often spend our whole lives pursuing things, status, and money, thinking that they're the ultimate end goal. But when we leave this earth, the only thing that really matters is no thing at all. What will matter is the experience of YOU that you leave behind with others. No one will care about how cool you were, how much money you had, what kind of car you drove, or what kinds of clothes you wore; people will remember how you made them FEEL.

The person we are today is creating the legacy that we will leave behind. With this in mind, we can be more intentional with our lives. We can strive to create lasting and loving memories with our family and friends, live from a place of joy and gratitude, and ultimately leave a mark on the world that we can be proud of. So how will you be remembered? What about you and your essence will forever be cherished?

Don't wait to become the person you've always dreamed of; be that person NOW.

YOUR MISSION: What are the three most important things that you want to be remembered for when your physical body leaves this earth?

1. _____

2. _____

3. _____

Today, and every day hereafter, live that legacy now. Strive to leave every single person you encounter with these three perspectives of you.

REFLECTION: What did you notice about yourself in this exercise? Are you proud of the legacy you're living right now? Or are you seeing that there are some changes you'd like to make?

_____

_____

_____

_____

_____

_____

_____

_____

_____

_____

_____

_____

_____

_____

_____

_____

Go forth with
PASSION.

#50WaysToYay

If you enjoyed this book, leave a review on Amazon or send me a little blurb about why you loved it, and I'll send you a sweet little thank-you gift for spreading the love.

Send a copy of the review or testimonial to bookreview@alexipanos.com so I know where to send your gift!

—Alexi

To get more goodness, check out my website:
www.alexipanos.com

THE **BRIDGE** METHOD

To sign up for my 12-Week Online Training Intensive,
THE BRIDGE METHOD, visit:
www.thebridgemethod.org.

For more information on my nonprofit, **E.P.I.C.**,
and my work in bringing clean water to those in need,
check out www.epicthemovement.org.

To apply for **E.P.I.C.'s Fellowship Program**
and lead your own service project abroad, please visit
www.epicfellowshipprogram.com.

ACKNOWLEDGMENTS

(READ TO THE END . . . I WROTE SOMETHING ABOUT YOU!)

This may be the hardest part of writing a book. I feel as if I'm overflowing with people to thank, as my entire life has been filled with so many incredible souls who have supported me on this journey and have had a significant impact on the person that I am today. I could write an entire book about how the people in my life have impacted and shaped me, but to save you from complete boredom, I'll keep it short and sweet.

First, I want to acknowledge my incredibly supportive family, who have always encouraged me to think outside the box and dance to the beat of my own drum. They set an incredible example for me, making sure that I knew that whatever I put my mind to, I could achieve with commitment, perseverance, and patience. I think of all the risks I've taken in life in starting different businesses, creating a nonprofit, and traveling the world, and it simply feels as if that's *what we do*. Thank you for creating a sense of ingenuity and adventure within me that has been guiding my journey since I was young. Thank you for being real, passionate (each in your own amazing way), and just a little bit crazy to always keep life interesting! I truly wouldn't be the woman I am today without the influence of you all: Mom, Dad, Steph, Kris, Stephanie, Marene, Yia Yia, Papou, Grandma Milne, Granddaddy, all the great-aunts and uncles, Pam, Pierre, Jack, Laurie, Bobbi, Scott, Robin; my cousins, who are like my brothers and sisters—Evan, Chanelle, Jourdan, Katrina, JT, Troy, Shane, Flynn, Ryan, and CJ. To all my little nephews and nieces—I'm so madly in love with you and over-the-moon that I get to watch you grow up! To Jackie, Preston Sr., Shalea, Winston, Skye, and Bubby—thank you for making me feel so welcomed from day one. I adore how loving, open, and real you all are, and I feel so blessed to call you my family! To my African family—you are truly EPIC! You have placed such an openness on my heart. Your love, your joy, your support of E.P.I.C., and your unwavering commitment to your community are inspiring. I love you guys!

To my Partner in Shine, Preston—you truly are magic. No words exist that can encapsulate all you are to me and to the world. You are such a gift, and I feel so blessed to be walking alongside you on this journey of life and service. I can't wait to grow old with you, build a ridiculously amazing family, and be the craziest old kids on the block. Thank you for always holding me to my highest self and supporting my shine whenever possible. Thank you for being a man of such amazing integrity. Thank you for being ALL of you. I love you.

To Jax—the one true modern-day gypsy woman I know. Thank you for being such a stand for love, truth, and beauty in the world. You and I have had such a magical ride in this life together, and I've loved living life to the max with you. Thank you for opening up my heart and showing me what love and authenticity is. Your impact on my life is immeasurable. Thank you for always taking the road less traveled; for being crazy, beautiful, and brilliant. You're the truth. Love you.

To Tennille—thank you for being my incredible partner with E.P.I.C., one of my best friends, and my sister (from another mister!). We have truly been through it all, and I absolutely love how we keep evolving who we are as individuals, as well as partners in impact, so that we can continue to serve the world as we feel called to do. Thank you for always being insanely committed to our friendship and always supporting me. I love you.

To my incredible friends, old and new—I cannot thank you enough for the impression you've left on my heart. We've gone through so much growth together, and I love how our friendships continue to open up my heart and my mind and to inspire and challenge me in so many ways. Thank you for being really exceptional people and standing for truth, service, and growth above all else. Thank you for being freaking awesome human beings and shining your incredible lights in my life! I absolutely love you.

To Bruce Cryer—thank you for being an incredible human being. Your warmth, spirit, love, and generosity are impeccable. Without you, this book would not be possible, and I'm truly grateful to know you. Thank you.

To Michele and Kathryn—thank you for being such rock stars! Thank you for believing in my message and for dealing with all of my last-minute additions! Thank you for creating a home for Preston and me to grow into and making us feel like family. I sincerely love what you both stand for and how committed you are to bringing work to the world that will have an impact and make a difference. And finally, thank you for both being hard-core New Yorkers. Every time I talk to you it reminds me of why I love New York City so much! Big thanks to every single rock star at North Star Way who helped bring this project to light—this truly was a team effort and your contribution was critical to making this happen!

To everyone who supported the launch of this book, your commitment to helping me spread this message has completely left me speechless. Your unwavering belief in this work and your encouragement along the way has meant the world to me, and I can't thank you enough for standing for my growth and expansion.

To my Tribe of Transformers out there—my Bridge Method and Bridge Experience family, my Naked Truth family, my Facebook, YouTube, and Instagram family: WOW! Thank YOU!!! You literally blow my heart wide open on a daily basis. Seriously, this book would not have been possible without you. Without your commitment to living your best life, standing strong in your authentic self, and shining your light out onto the world, this work wouldn't have been created. You continue to inspire so much goodness in me to keep sharing, keep standing in my own truth, and keep encouraging others to do the same. There are so many of you I feel I know because of the incredible messages we exchange (even though we've never met), and there are so many of you that I've had the honor and privilege of meeting (and hugging the crap out of!) that I feel instantly bonded to. THANK YOU. Thank you for welcoming me into a part of your lives and always supporting me. Thank you for standing for yourselves to live a powerful and authentic life. Thank you for standing for the greatness of every single human being on this planet. And thank you for taking a stand for LOVE. Your voice matters, and I sincerely believe that *we* are creating a massive shift in the world with our love and our light. NEVER stop showing up as love and shining that beautiful light of yours!

Finally, I would like to give gratitude for life. As I write this,

I'm feeling overwhelmed by just how blessed my life truly is and how there is so much magic in this world. I'm honored to be alive during this time and I'm incredibly grateful to have a voice that I am able to use for good. I am truly blessed and so grateful to be here, now.

Well played, Universe, well played.

ABOUT THE AUTHOR

Alexi Panos has inspired and empowered hundreds of thousands of people toward a life of personal fulfillment through her various speaking, workshop, multimedia, and philanthropic platforms. As cofounder of the transformational methodology called The Bridge Method, she is making waves all over the world for its revolutionary new take on radical self-development. Alexi is also the cofounder of the nonprofit E.P.I.C. (Everyday People Initiating Change), which has provided clean water and community development for tens of thousands of people in the developing world since 2005. Named as one of *Origin* magazine's Top 100 Creatives Changing the World, winner of *Elixir* magazine's Millennial Mentor Award, and dubbed one of "11 Noteworthy Millennials" in the *Huffington Post*, Alexi is truly shaking things up with her passionate and energetic delivery, making a unique mark on the world.